# ANGEL MIND

## EANE HUFF

**Different View Productions**

Angel Mind
All Rights Reserved.
Copyright © 2019 Eane Huff
v1.0

The opinions expressed in this manuscript are solely the opinions of the author and do not represent the opinions or thoughts of the publisher. The author has represented and warranted full ownership and/or legal right to publish all the materials in this book.

This book may not be reproduced, transmitted, or stored in whole or in part by any means, including graphic, electronic, or mechanical without the express written consent of the publisher except in the case of brief quotations embodied in critical articles and reviews.

Different View Productions

ISBN: 978-0-578-22556-2

Cover Photo © 2019 Eane Huff. All rights reserved - used with permission.

PRINTED IN THE UNITED STATES OF AMERICA

# Table of Contents

**CONNECTING** ............................................................................................................... 1

    The Human Condition ................................................................................................ 3

    Programs to Discover ................................................................................................ 4

    Chains of Liberation and Freedom ............................................................................ 6

    Connecting With the Source of Angel-Mind .............................................................. 7

    The Many Faces of God ............................................................................................ 8

    Prayer-Activity Leading to Proactivity ..................................................................... 10

    Merging Science and Spirituality ............................................................................ 11

    Billions of Years Can't Be Wrong ............................................................................ 11

    An Age of Absence ................................................................................................. 12

    A Search for the Angel Within ................................................................................ 12

    The Angel-Mind ...................................................................................................... 13

    Role Models ............................................................................................................ 13

    Dimensions of Reality ............................................................................................. 15

    Angel-Mind Role Models Showing the Way ............................................................ 17

    The Brain: An Old Model That is Holding Humanity Back ...................................... 18

    The Window ........................................................................................................... 22

    The Two Hemispheres of Angel-Mind Contributing Unified Meaning ..................... 22

    Vertical Integration ................................................................................................. 24

    The God Circuit ...................................................................................................... 25

    Building Faith ................................................................................................................. 26

    "God, Make Me an Angel" ............................................................................................ 27

    Present and Accounted for ............................................................................................ 27

    Agency ........................................................................................................................... 29

## LIVING YOUR MESSAGE ................................................................................................... 33

    Finding God--A Choice of Lemons or Limes ................................................................. 34

    The Message Inside ....................................................................................................... 34

    Destiny or Development? .............................................................................................. 36

    CLAP Your Hands Together in Prayer ............................................................................ 37

    Seeking Spirit ................................................................................................................. 37

    Experiencing and Expressions of Angel-Message .......................................................... 38

    Finding a Pathway to Becoming .................................................................................... 40

    The Destiny of Angel-Mind ............................................................................................ 41

    God's Reflection ............................................................................................................ 42

    Revolution Angel-Mind .................................................................................................. 43

    Angel-Minds Revealing Themselves ............................................................................... 43

    God Is an Individual Gift ................................................................................................ 44

    Soul (Sole) Work ............................................................................................................ 44

    The World Waiting to Receive ....................................................................................... 45

    The Message Sent and a Response Is Guaranteed ........................................................ 46

    Right Message, Right Time ............................................................................................ 46

    No Death—Angel-Mind Lives on With Effort, Protection, and Advocacy ..................... 47

## THE FLIGHT ....................................................................................................................... 49

    Self-Regulation Is the Key to Experience God's Message and Understand It ................ 50

Individual and God-Given Greatness .................................................................. 50

Angel-Mind for the Times .................................................................................. 51

Angel Mind Crying Out Loud ............................................................................. 51

Addictions .......................................................................................................... 52

Discovering the Inner Angel .............................................................................. 53

Clear Communication ....................................................................................... 54

Finding the Angel Within ................................................................................... 55

The Persistence of Angels ................................................................................. 55

Dividing and Divining Angels in a Secular Society ........................................... 56

Forgot…or for God? ........................................................................................... 58

Darkening Skies ................................................................................................ 59

A Steady Flight .................................................................................................. 60

THE [R]EVOLUTION .............................................................................................. 63

Becoming ........................................................................................................... 64

Angels Remember: Isn't It Time for Gabrielle's Law? ....................................... 65

Angel-Mind Overcoming Trauma ...................................................................... 67

A Silent Angel .................................................................................................... 68

Discovering the Inner Angel .............................................................................. 69

# CONNECTING

Let me contribute in the way that only I have been made to…

## THE HUMAN CONDITION

The human frame is a fragile container for the immense potential and possibility that we hold as individuals. While the lifespan of humanity may seem to be abbreviated compared to the individual jobs we each have to do, it is not too big an order for all of us. Angel-Mind is what combines everyone together. Each individual has the choice to operate with their highest abilities. With the highest abilities and God's direction, the best things happen. Angel-Mind allows fundamental God-Values to protect and to elevate those who use and need it.

Angelhood was once reserved for exceptional cases of individuals who found themselves able to attain the highest functioning. Establishing societal advances that we all rely on advanced society to where it is currently. Now the present is becoming a new challenge. The world and the people within it now depend on Angels and their messages. Overpopulation, climate change, and human angst have contributed to an uncertain future. Angel-Mind is needed more than ever.

Society is dependent on the God-Values that each individual has to deliver in a personal demonstration of applied learning and being. While logic has seemed to drown out the need for God in life, the heart and mind still yearn for a relationship with God. Seen in the advancements of society and the breakthroughs that are relied on, from intricate brain surgery that separates conjoined twins to the invention of the toilet, nothing is too mundane or specialized for Angel-Mind. Each development that has come from Angel-Mind has improved lives and changed human living potential. When each of us chooses to contribute our highest abilities and care for each other, we are linked together by God and Angel-Mind. God-Values and the highest abilities will guide us into the unknown. When God is present in our lives, survival of the human race and the earth is assured. Every Angel-Mind has contributed ideas and leadership to help save society. Problems have been solved by Angel-Mind with the application of logic and creativity to produce convincing solutions. By delivering each individual message with the spirit and highest abilities we are born with, we change the existence of humanity.

But the belief of how we can allow ourselves to connect with God, one of the most important relationships in our life, gets obscured by situations that are overwhelming to the individual. Contribution, one of the most essential and important God-Values, reflects God's plans, because with Angel-Mind He has made all things possible and dependent on what we each do, from saving this world to being able to protect those in need. Each individual is made to contribute a part of the message as Angels rely upon each other. The messages and identities each of us hold make up the face of God. Each Angel-Mind that completes God's plan is proof that God does exist. Each action motivated by Angel-Mind is part of God's plan.

The frailty of the human form is not something that cannot be taken lightly. Each life that is lived by Angel-Mind, each energy of contribution, leadership, advocacy, or protection is just one way that each Angel-Mind lives on. Each Angel that uses Angel-Mind to support life and allow better living carries on with the energy invested another individual. The energy and gratitude of the individual who finds a better day to participate in and is more prepared to live life is an example of the investment that has been given by the Angel-Mind that cared for the individual. Angels who use Angel-Mind live forever, because the vibrations of their message continue to resound in others. Angels' unique gifts benefit the human race and continue to resound within those who choose to remember.

## Programs to Discover

The intricacies of the genetic code represent programs for greatness or developing challenges. Each segment of DNA interweaves the needs and wants of humanity. Every person has a unique personality and genetic code that reveals their messages and purposes in their life. Their personality will express connections with God that will contribute to each situation. The purposes of each human can be revealed as they gain skills that guide their life and abilities. God, as the most patient, skilled, and masterful Watchmaker, meticulously constructs cogs within the helixes of different DNA segments that will influence development of the world and its inhabitants. God watches and smiles, recording each Angel-Mind's success and brainstorming for the next Angel-Mind that the world needs to contribute to it and maintain it. A complicated recipe is followed, one that allows each of His creations to make the meaningful decision of depending on themselves, supporting another, depending on another's support, or contributing to this world. Angel-Minds who find they want to contribute and who yearn to serve may find life positions providing assistance to those who need. As Angel-Minds, the programming and message will be discovered in a myriad of ways--a close relationship as someone's advocate, a teacher, an official for the city you live in, or even a customer service associate.

Each individual's programming in their life, the double helixes that influence the development of characteristics, or challenging life situations may be a reason to find your angel. These interconnections of needs weave all of humanity together. Every situation presents an opportunity for Angel-Mind to serve its purpose. The inspirational leader connects with the individual who feels bored with life, the engaging therapist connects with the individual who needs to discover the abilities that will let them succeed. An individual who finds they need help with an electrical problem in their house may make a call to a skilled electrician who has become qualified by developing their abilities to a high degree. Angel-Mind is everywhere, residing within needs or providing assistance. All of humanity is the biggest jigsaw puzzle, each person locking and fitting into the place of someone needing assistance, or providing help for another. Each person will find themselves needing, nurturing, supporting, or protecting another during their life experiences, providing insight into God's plan. Other Angel-Minds, born without the yearning to serve, may decide to work with highly trained and independent employees to show their best work. Still other individuals may decide their life is best expressed in solitary existence. The choice to depend on one another will be a culmination of life experiences. Depending on another, the Angel-pairing contributes to each other's existence. Finding each other's needs and complementing, the aspects of Angel-Mind benefits each individual and the world. That is God's way of Angel-Mind.

Each Angel-Mind has a unique sense of God's timing. The placement of where an individual is at can make the critical difference between being a pedestrian who unknowingly walks into the path of a speeding car and being the pedestrian who is able to restrain that same pedestrian with a strong hand that grips their shoulder. That action changes their life, and they find that one of their God-Values programmed within them is protection.

Timing also deals with the decision of when you have found your message. An elderly woman, never finding much time to do anything else than take care of family, enjoys celebrating her birthday when she is surprised by her extended family that shows up. She decides in the twilight of her life that her message and actions of cooking meals, assisting young children with homework, and being someone who was always trying to help the family, was advocacy—the God-Value she operated with.

Experiences can affect programming. Be aware that programs which we are born with and God is excited to watch manifest into remarkable Angel-abilities may be altered from their original construction by an anomaly in environmental conditions or the process of development. As Angels who feel drawn to God's plan, it is important to persist through with the changes in self so that the Angel continues. Angel-Mind carries the same message God created each of us with, regardless of how we change. The message may be delivered by a different method but will carry the same resonance, which will affect those it has been made for.

As humans who find multiple possibilities within themselves, the programming within each individual may have different aspects and can be seen different ways. The individual using the God-Value of protection to save the walker could easily look at themselves as using the God-Value of leadership. Individuals who choose to look at themselves differently can receive the gift of gaining abilities that accompany a new level of confidence. Angel-Minds choosing to look at themselves as a leader would amplify their life message and presence.

Each Angel-Mind must decide for themselves if there is a time to decide what message they operate with or rely on, living according to their programming and that turns into their life message. Each individual is set up to have an individual experience, from a chronic disorder or disability that points an individual to needing an Angel, or the yearning to serve prompting the discovery of a hidden interest to help others. An individual can go through life with a sense of wonder in experiencing God's plans and timing, discovering each part of their life as a part of serving God. If they need assistance or support to achieve a dream, the need shows God's plan for further development of Angel-Mind or for an Angel of Advocacy to be discovered. The existence of Angel-Mind is to allow each individual to be of service to humanity. If that means reliance upon another because of some need, the Angel or services that can help that individual already exists, is developing, or has been developed and is refining.

By contributing, supporting and leading, directing and protecting so that an individual benefits from Angel-Mind, programs within ourselves are discovered—programs that tell Angel-Mind where it needs to be and what it is designed to do. It reveals what God designed Angel-Mind to do: contribute to the individuals of this earth.

Discovering and adjusting to the programs that are developing within can be one of the biggest challenges for Angel-Mind. Expectations and reactions about changes to individual abilities influences acceptance of life conditions and the emotion associated with those changes. Dependence on others may be required to bring the best opportunities for Angel-Mind to develop. Finding solace may be another option, depending on God's plan.

Individual choices change Angel-Mind potential and ability. Relating highly to personal situations and the constraints felt about those situations, Angel-Mind can be hampered by the personal experiences and situations that are entered into. As each individual goes through their programs or experiences anomalies that weren't planned for, God watches, records, and places ultimate faith in Angel-Mind. God waits for the [R]evolution of humans caring about the earth and His creations to begin. Our place with God begins when Angel-Mind is used to amplify and elevate existence, increasing the ability to a better relationship with God, increasing caring and understanding for humanity.

## Chains of Liberation and Freedom

Have you ever wondered how many people have contributed to your life, or how many Angels have actually encouraged you or spurred you on to your success? Chains of Angels have contributed to the success and liberation which have enabled humans to find their success and enjoy a better life. I have depended on Angels throughout my life. Angels with steady hands, who have performed delicate brain repairs and incisions with their bandages and scalpels and used masterful repairing touches they learned from others that have let me come back from life-threatening brain injuries. Therapeutic touch has restored my ability to do what I do and to more fully contribute what I can. Two head injuries and a realization that I have overcome my own limitations have made me search for and realize that there is more to this world than just tangible experiences. The Angels who have worked with me and contributed their understandings of what the best life directions and therapies were for me have convinced me that Angels do exist.

How many chains of Angels did it take for you to find your success in life? I have found my message being linked to the hands of doctors performing life-saving operations on me and learned from inspirational leaders who have convinced me that a much deeper connection of understanding and being who I can be is available to me. Teachers have guided and encouraged me in ways that were unnoticeable to a beginning learner's eye. Observing what is happening in the world and realizing the number of people who are disenfranchised convinces me that an [R]evolution is what is needed to change the world we are living in now.

Angel-Mind's message and power may be ultimately altered by the experiences that happen to each of us. Science says I have overcome trauma by a mutation in my genes that makes me resistant to trauma's effects. A Master's Degree in Diversity Education from Western Oregon University that took nine years to complete convinces me that I have worked with amazing Angels who were predisposed to help me succeed while I underwent internal struggles to find my wings. Now, I find myself amazed and perplexed by the achievements I have made and completed, the piece of life that I find myself fitting into. It was not just me who made these achievements. Others took part in my accomplishment, sharing their own message, discovering and exercising their own Angel, relying on their own skills that they developed and which allowed them to excel.

Each brain cell pulsing with the same communication, each individual's message adding to and reinforcing the messages of others that had already taken root made me become who I am. Each transaction represented the living message that God placed in each individual. Messages being nurtured by experiences and growing with repeated practice of successful routines allow each individual to develop the Angel-Mind that we are each born to develop. And with practice, we may end up to represent the Angels that God made us to be.

Others' highest thinking allowed them to discover thoughts of Angel-Mind. It is what God truly wants us all to engage in and what we each are blessed with. The four concepts of Angel-Mind, each made to protect and help those who may need it, are some of the most magnificent tools of God. Every person who uses Angel-Mind, and participates in higher thinking and ability, is proof that God exists and is why we can have hope as we move forward in life. Angel-Mind allows humans to have freedom to exist and develop their passions, with the ultimate goal of saving each other and contributing to God's plan.

## Connecting With the Source of Angel-Mind

But who, or what, is God? The greatest epiphany that can happen is that there will never be any proof of God, except for realization that because we exist with the ability to use Angel-Mind and rely on Angel-Mind advances, God is with us and makes up who we are. Our actions bring caring and protection, and will result in being the saving grace of humanity. God has designed it that way. Each of us can use Angel-Mind to encourage the ultimate achievement and manifestations of who we have the ability to be. Demonstrating Angel-Mind, we can all be an example of God's Angels, caring for each other and protecting and leading those that need to be led and protected. We each have existed or do exist to allow our own message of God to exist and have the possibility of God's message to change others. The human race is the manifestation of God, and the [R]evolution of Angel-Mind is how God will be found. The proof of God rests on us. We have waited long enough for God to find us; now it's time to find Him. What actions do you look at as representative of how God would want us to relate to the earth and each other?

## *The Many Faces of God*

Each experience and every word in our dictionary can describe God, as each individual using Angel-Mind brings the message of God into experience. All behavior reflects an attempt at discovering or revealing God, yet all behaviors are not successful in achieving a relationship with God or discovering and using God-Values. Every dictionary describes God. God is beyond human comprehension, and yet, rooted in each human as a life message, God resounds in each one of us and in how we behave. The behavior exhibited by some humans may be outside of the influence of God. As humans who use Angel-Mind, the choice to behave for God or against God is always an option. A concerted and conscious choice to use or not to use Angel-Mind demonstrates behavior that is helpful and nurturing to humans and the world or hurtful or discouraging to humans and the world. Empowering, caring, supporting, inspiring, virtuous, potential-releasing, and potential-infusing all are words that can describe humans as deliverers of God's unique message and who are trying to fulfill programs that are inside of them. The counterpoint to God's message of goodness, however, are individuals who discover faulty programs within and represent evil, incestuous, vindictive, malicious, raping, bullying, or victimizing behavior. Despite the wicked interpretations and descriptions of the behavior of humans who are running faulty programs, we are all reliant upon God's messages and the developments from Angels that have come before us.

God has given humans the choice to find and support Godly messages. Expression of the gender of God changes, as it should. What role does God play in your current view? If God is nurturing, life-giving, and encouraging, that could easily be a pronoun described by, "she," yet there may be a perspective where "he" could be used as well. Boundaries, limits, and rules, stereotypically a family role demonstrated by fathers, could be "he," yet there could be examples where "she" would apply. There is no correct gender for God, except the way in which you experience God. Is there a gender role that you feel better working with or working for? Because, as Angels who use Angel-Mind, we do all work for God....

The situations and the present that face each of us will be different for all and can vary widely upon which hemisphere you are looking out of. The possibilities God represents can be expressed by the beautiful gleaming sunlight peeking above the horizon as you look out your window in the morning, observing the beautiful portrait of God's peaceful, gentle visage. Or another portrait might be waking in the night to observe the unbridled anger of a severe coastal storm and experiencing the dread you hold within while you worry about your family as they sleep through the night. These portraits of God's faces are all revealing, and how we see the visage of God influences human behavior. The smile you have as you put on your favorite warm socks during a cold morning influences your experiences of the emotional landscape and can expose a spiritual window. Think of how many times your feelings have opened up connections of closeness between you and another. The rapport and opportunities for closeness are influenced by how our experiences prepare our Angel-Mind to be receptive to a message or to reject it. Think of caring for a family pet, or a home renovation that you have participated in. The endeavors that are invested in and the feelings of success we experience result in and influence a different face of God. Each of the Angel-Mind's hemisphere specialization determines what we will see and the path that will be followed to achieve God's message within.

Facing the future might look like taking responsibility for a situation by proactively finding a way to respond to a situation that has been haltingly affecting your life. Behavior combining with thoughts representative of the message that God puts in each of us contribute, modify, and reinforce humanity to unite us with the Angels that we need to meet, learn from, and release the Angel-Mind that is waiting to serve.

Remember the civic discourse, discussion, and possibilities planted in the human consciousness when the quote "Random Acts of Kindness" entered societal awareness and gained focus? Angels were released, and messages of goodness and helping came alive in society! Strangers who didn't know each other discovered programming and spirit that helped them heal each other.

Society's illusion of separateness was overcome. Angels that were hiding in the souls of people found their wings and took flight. People started taking action in effort to represent an enhanced representation of God's caring and influence. The [R]evolution of humanity is coming, and for those of us who are keenly aware of the moment, we are constructing the thoughts, prayers, and awareness to facilitate the movement.

Human progress and learning have rested on the wings of Angels. Inventors and scientists have been describing and interpreting how God looks to each of us; their inventions because of Angel-Mind have sustained us. The concept of change over the development of the earth has changed our potential survival rate to be the best it could be against predators or enemies.

With brains that could change and adapt to challenges presented by predators, humans found an evolutionary advantage produced by Angel-Mind. Each person is blessed with a brain that is uniquely different from everyone else's, offering different survival advantages. But while human communication has let each human profit from another human's expertise, the isolation of humans from God's message, protection, and love has not enhanced society. Evolution and species change are now facing a tipping point. People either are needing to change now, without depending on evolutionary changes that will enhance survivability, or we all face extinction. The [R]evolution of

Angel-Mind is humanity's best solution for survival.

Overpopulation, climate change, wildlife displacement, and food growth techniques all indicate planet health and show how unprepared each individual is to meet challenges that are manifesting today, leaving humanity exposed to extinction. Overexpansion is leading to the death of other species on earth that need to be preserved as a function of global health.

Evolution will not prepare the individual for the changes it needs to make. "Fight or flight" survival strategies, once useful to avoid predators, grow unneeded as society has been regulated to protect life. Strategies of God-sight and revival of working with God's message and essence are the new survival skills that must be learned. Evolution is taking too long to address the challenges of humanity, yet a [R]evolution in humanity is not impossible or improbable. By relying on each individual that is on this earth as a potential contributor to help humanity survive, we may just have a chance.

Humans who have used Angel-Mind have brought humanity and its advancements to where it is currently. God has many faces, and we each are brought closer to God when using Angel-Mind. Every individual is representative of the face of God.

## *Prayer-Activity Leading to Proactivity*

Prayer is God's language. Each moment of gratitude that can be celebrated or moment of consternation that humans endure needs to prayed about and to be recognized. That recognition of the situation will enhance Angel-Mind's ability to address it and will bring the best of outcomes. Gratitude is the fuel of Angel-Mind, and can lead to the best and most adaptive thoughts which can change society. The problem, challenge, or celebration needs to be put into the subconscious. The brain understands God-language and is where Angel-Mind comes from, which hasn't been used since the time we started drawing away from God. Reuniting with God-Values and instructions, Angel-Minds benefit from prayer. The calming effects of prayer allow individual connections to slow-down, take needed action, find insight, and follow direction. Each individual shares a direct connection with God, and our prayers allow spiritual resonance.

Brain messages, each energized by resolve to act how God needs us to, proactivity and prayer-activity both change humans into the ultimate spiritual mechanics. Each individual working to help protect, lead, and celebrate humanity like their God-given message tells them to grow with healing and change. Prayer may need to be engaged in several times before it produces action, but aligning with God's intent and purpose, each person will find the time to care for and inspire Angel-Mind advances. By using the mind's body and brains that so clearly resonate with God, we become Angels ourselves.

## *Merging Science and Spirituality*

Brain research and scientific information are each a gift from the researchers who have found a passion for research into the history of our brain and changing world. Research that not only challenges existing thoughts but also demonstrates a higher understanding of the benefits of Angel-Mind may find a useful or meaningful application in thinking and evaluating topics of concern. Adding to an understanding of how we can each play a part in the changing world of knowledge and Angel ability, reliance and modification upon previous Angel-Minds' work, gifts, and messages are what God wants. Each Angel contributing to a better understanding and knowledge base is what God intended. A chain reaction of fluttering wings, the passion each Angel-Mind has to contribute to humanity means the best of spirituality and scientific application hold greater fulfillment, meaning, and purpose for each Angel-Mind.

Many answers are available in this world of knowledge, and many perspectives. There are so many different points of view that contributing research, voicing opinions, and engaging in discussions with other Angel-Minds will be the only way to experience truth and realize conclusions. Angel-Mind offers different realities depending on the window that is looked out of to perceive reality. All of these answers can be correct, yet the answers that truly resonate with you, the ones that stir your soul, are the right Angel-Message for you.

## *Billions of Years Can't Be Wrong*

God continues to be with us, to choose to accompany us and be overjoyed by our successes and how learning occurs with mistakes. God cheers on His creations despite our overuse and misdistribution. God waits for us to learn to regulate and share, to become the Angels that She always planned on us to become. The [R]evolution of humanity has come to a standstill: we are not showing any adaptive changes that will increase survival or ability to exist. We are at the highest stage of evolution of our species. Yet, we are not yet taking care of each other as we need to. The [R]evolution of Angel-Mind, while not dealing with any physical changes that will enhance survival, does have to do with mental changes that will result in changing the human race's survival.

Agreeing, acknowledging, and resolving that Angel-Mind is the first step to starting our flight with God is a priority to finding the brilliance of Angel-Mind. God's many faces show how each Angel delivers the message. There may be many messages that resound inside the souls of those who are predisposed toward Angel-Mind. The promise of Angels connecting with society and the culture within it is how we all can succeed. The true gift is the presence and ability that has been shown by the many faces of God and sculpted by the message within.

## An Age of Absence

Society has found an addiction within the possibilities offered by the world. Rather than communicating with one person, now it is possible to communicate in multiple ways that seduces people into thinking that they are being present with the people who need the attention or acknowledgement of an individual. With more communications to add complication to an existing relationship, technology is diminishing the power of Angel-Mind.

Technology has amplified the goodwill of Angels in an amazing way by encouraging and simplifying donation and helping-behavior. But the complex realization of reduced human contact must be taken into account. Only by stepping outside of the technological landscape will humanity be nurtured. Technology can certainly be a factor that adds to the medium of the developing message of self, but the real present of Angel-Mind is the gift that will change humanity and encourage building greatness. Which brings you closer to a person, a handwritten note or typed one? A homemade card or a store-bought card? An e-mailed message or a hand-delivered envelope? The closeness of Angel-Mind rests on the delivery of self.

Presence in this age of absence is an essential skill of being able to respond and interact with a situation. Inviting the rewards of presence is an exciting and rewarding experience. By staying focused, you encourage Angel-Mind to become the leader and what the moment needs.

Being present with a situation or individual is one of the needs and demands of Angel-Mind. Angel-Mind exists and supports God when attention is brought to all consequences of a situation, both intended and unintended. Being in a state of receiving vital feedback from both allows Angel-Mind to know that it is having the effects it strives to have and is minimizing the negative effects. This state of fluidity is what allows Angel-Mind to serve vital demographics and to find a place for each to fit into the interlocking puzzle of the world. Listening to and incorporating the needs and messages of individuals allows the faces of God to be truly seen. Angel-Mind is truly blessed when staring into God's many faces.

## A Search for the Angel Within

Angel-Mind deals with flourishing and finding a way that each of us will prosper and save ourselves by allowing individuals new and better ways to contribute to society. It deals with God's plan and the Angels that can and will change and influence society. Angels and Angel-Mind are all around us, yet many don't realize the potential each individual has, which can contribute God's message. Finding the Angel-Mind that is located within, competition and striving for accolades subsides, replaced by contribution and connection. Soul work and passions that reveal individual gifts are emphasized, and the holistic health of all will be considered and prioritized.

Society has convinced each individual that they are working against each other, and in that process, the addition of the individual messages that we each can contribute to society are minimized in their potential. No message too small, no thought too simple; Angel-Mind is something that can and does change society.

## THE ANGEL-MIND

God and Angel-Mind are found all around the world. Each moment, another chance is allowed to discover how important Angel-Mind is and how it has changed society. The leadership from Angel-Mind provides the best messages to fit in this jigsaw puzzle of humanity. Angel-Mind gives indications and recognition that we each have response patterns and messages that are programmed by God. These messages are lived out in entirety or satisfied partially, depending on how long it has taken to develop and adhere to Angel-Mind concepts. Think of the altruism that many people don't even realize they are programmed with. When another person is struggling, the natural human program is to want to help. The programs are within our DNA and have become such a natural part of being human that they are called human nature. The communication programming has allowed each Angel-Mind to be a contributor to God's plan by relying on each other's expertise which has been essential in developing excellence and living better. Another important factor are programs of friendliness, which have encouraged people to walk a careful line that allows reciprocity, combining interests, and developing commonality. Friendship is a gift given by God that requires an individual's timing and purpose to be shared by another with similar yearnings for friendship and communication. By operating with Angel-Mind, those programs help change society.

How we see ourselves can reflect societal approval of the position that each individual operates from. Whether it is from a position of homelessness and illiteracy or a position of celebrity and affluence, Angel-Mind sees the needs of everyone. Everyone needs balance, help, guidance, and protection, a feeling of acknowledgement and contribution, and to be included in society. To truly engage in the saving of the world and its inhabitants, each Angel-Mind needs to engage with society. Each person's story holds meaning and worth and will allow answers to be found and produced. How we allow ourselves to respond and advocate for each individual determines our flight path. Angel-Mind contribution could mean deciding that a book drive and reading instruction programs need to be established to help fight illiteracy, or the possibility of homeless shelters needs to be brought up and petitioned for at the next City Hall meeting.

## ROLE MODELS

By showing examples of Angels that have changed society and affected the understanding of human nature, Angels are proven to exist. In fact, Angels have been significant in humans' understanding and survival on this earth. Each Angel-Mind who has served humanity with positive expressions of caring, contribution, leadership, advocacy, and protection which amounted to magnificent gains in quality of life of those who are dependent on Angel-Mind. Angel-Mind behavior allows role models to be established, which allow possibilities to be understood regarding what humans using Angel-Mind can actually become. Goodness comes from the messages of Angels, resounding with God's rapport that nurtures every one of us. Reliance on Angels and Angel-Mind demonstrates God's existence. God encourages our evolution and understanding of things to a higher level. Examples in this book make God smile and continue to have faith that humanity is changing and evolving from where it started. Evolution is needed by humans, and is why role models of Angel-Minds are important to learn from. Evolution is the proof that Angel-Mind is adapting to the new challenges of this world. Processing, understanding, and applying a higher level of engaging in the world's problems and needs allows a better world to be lived in and enjoyed. The individuals who are mentioned in this book are the Angel-Minds that have found a way of operating that restores God's creations and renews the blessings we share by being connected with Her.

Connections shared within the context of the culture is such a big factor in demonstrating the expanse of Angel-Mind. Carl Rogers found a message inside that changed the counselling world and how people were listened to and understood by finding a message inside himself that wanted to help people. Sigmund Freud also found he wanted to help people. Different contexts of the society each lived in resulted in two completely different messages regarding how the best counselling was performed. Rogers was using Angel-Mind when he chose counselling techniques that connected with people, where Freud chose static assumptions that conflicted with human spirit, giving him a reduced view of humanity. Only time told which Angel-Mind was more successful, but the differences in each Angel-Mind's message were easily shown. The context of each culture the message developed in and programs that were run demonstrated the success of each Angel-Mind.

Another Angel-Mind shows the power of a message divinely crafted. Martin Luther King Jr. led crowds of his followers to meticulously follow him through oppression and inhumane circumstances to emerge as a victorious leader who changed Civil Rights. His followers were also in the Angel-Mind state, because without them and their control, they couldn't make the statement that needed to be made. Spellbinding speaking and celebrated leadership existed only because Angels who chose to follow the message were ready to hear it existed. The Angels' gift was new ways to view humanity and understand Civil Rights.

Less well-known Angel-Minds might be your personal favorites who specialized in your specific work or interests. Dan Allendar's message resounds with those who have suffered from abuse and needed his books to become familiar with the process of healing and thriving. Sylvia Plath's insightful poetry and Nora Ephron's humorous storytelling developed into styles that have entertained readers and has shown how people want and will flock to works that come from Angel-Mind. Millions of books come from Angel-Mind, designed to entertain or heal others with a message developed from the writer's soul work.

Humanity's end goal is the [R]evolution of Angel-Mind. Angels have engaged in helping spread their messages and advances that they have within them. Each Angel-Mind, joined together by God's purpose, completes the jigsaw puzzle of humanity to add one more step to completion of finally discovering the Heaven we can all live in. Think of it! The signals that humanity is ready to depend on and reveal our divine nature is demonstrated with each act of humanity that does not reflect His values.

## *Dimensions of Reality*

The brain is unconsciously aware of God. Every moment that becomes an opportunity, every insight that has led to an advantage, is because of Angel-Mind. Yet because there are so many points of reference that are in the attentional spectrum, God's relevance is obscured. Sensory use has slowed the realization of God.

Angel-Mind connects all humans that are willing to exist in the possibility of being an Angel. It instills those who are willing to have an intention to connect to God-Values. The seed of Angel-Mind and the actions behind Angels, God-Values are the values that have become experientially activated or we internally know. These God-Values will guide your Angel-Mind's flight and the message you will personally contribute to society by being a representative of God.

Every one of society's advances, every one of its leaders, "good," or "bad," has existed because of Angel-Mind. As Angels, we each have the power to change our situations. Through life and living, we have each found the wishes we have and what we could provide. Statements that start with "God, if you could just bring back my friend who died a year ago today," provide a reminder of what your Angel-Mind needs and wants: a reunion with that friend who was taken from you that fateful day exactly one year ago. Death and loss are not events to take something from you that you once had; they are to remind you how precious life is. They also tell you that right now, that relationship you had and the feelings you experienced when you were in that relationship are something you need. Angel-Mind can bring back that feeling you treasured. Start looking for your friend purposefully. The next day, as the sun rises in the morning, you find your friend in the clouds, and you wrap your arms around the rays of sunshine that wrap around you. You say longingly, "I've missed you so much, my friend. It's great you're here." Shadows of our memories exist for more than remembrance of the special people in our life; they exist so that we can see each other again. With Angel-Mind, it is all possible.

The pain we have felt during our lives, the need for affiliation that we have felt longing in our soul, or the hurt and aggression that was lived with which directed us to act out with violence are some of the programs that life instills within which greatly affect Angel-potential. The choice whether to react against the experiences or choose to proactively deal with them is what Angels are born to do. Each Angel-Mind is born by an individual feeling the need to contribute, lead, and become who we are meant to be with advocacy and protection. Each Angel-Mind is meant to contribute their own message in a special way. Leadership may not first be identifiable with Angel-Mind; it can actually be the choice to lead by following. Yet Angel-Minds are the developers of greatness, nurturers of goodness, and experts at finding the strength within others. Whether it is the nurturing the development of growing Angel-Minds as a school cook, or becoming a millionaire from an invention in technology that everyone needs, Angel-Mind is being the best one can be and being the protector of those in need. Angel-Mind is the breathtaking ability that each individual is able to access by slowing down, directing focus, and concentrating on the God-Values each of us has within.

Participation in society and contributing is an essential part of Angel-Mind which leads to the cohesion in a society. Each individual has programs inside that want to be valued and appreciated. The larger society we have, the more important for Angel-Mind to acknowledge individual contributions that others have made.

God is within each of us, running through the blood we have and the thoughts that lead us or the thoughts that are pushed away. Angel-Mind is instilled with the leadership made to guide our society through the steps or missteps we take to achieve a better society. The actions we take either serve as actions and images of what God wants and intends, or they do not. The brain often stays on the border of discovery, knowing God is accessible, yet humans always may feel isolated because of the window they look out from. A natural symptom of the logical window which humans operate from, it will take a [R]evolution for humans to realize the spiritual workplace and life God has designed for each of us. Until humans have gained trust in themselves and the message they are born to give and receive, God waits, and listens, and smiles.

Dreams are a curious reminder of the supernatural and how the brain is called to process and develop higher abilities with Angel-Mind. Dreams are a constant reminder of how the world has God within, if we choose Angel-Mind and a higher state of connecting to ourselves. Dreams represent a mind interacting with opportunities presented by the environment. The brain processes many more stimuli than we are consciously aware of. Dreams are a feedback mechanism of all those stimuli. They must be decoded by the dreamer, and they will carry emotional resonance that will give you encouragement to continue the life message chosen or to realize that the path you are travelling is not for you. The most spectacular dreams that show untapped possibilities are the dreams that show God is here, waiting for each of our specific messages to develop and see if God and the Angel-Minds we each have a chance to access will save the world.

## *Angel-Mind Role Models Showing the Way*

When you can see your development, experience, and existence as the result of the special tutelage and existence of role models who have shown the way, that is when the Angel-Mind connection becomes extraordinary. Who would make up the links of the chains of special Angels who have affected and affect your life? Every development that has come to exist is a product of Angel-Mind. Some Angel-Minds that support others may have no intention of being recognized, but they have been blessed with the wings that have let them fly and find success. They are content with the abilities they have that allow them to contribute and heal society. It is time to think about the angels that have come before us, for no other reason than just to acknowledge that Angel-Mind exists, it resounds and beats with success, and it is present in our society. Every invention that we have come to rely on has appeared from Angel-Mind and is a reminder of our unique relationship with God. The individuals who subsist with Angel-Mind, who resound with their messages of Angel-Mind, change lives. The college professor who spent extra time in college to foster relational and logical understanding of the concepts he taught, the supermarket Angel who always changes my day with her conversation and attention, barista Angels who effortlessly fill my Iced Americano while engaging in conversation with me all contribute to a special feeling of family and connection. All these examples demonstrate an application of Angel-Mind. Angel-Mind becomes very evident and is a present to be celebrated in life.

Another Angel, a counselor who actually helped me develop Angel-Mind by example, encourages me to concentrate on my personal development and application. Angels change lives with the unique message that resounds within them. By delivering their message, they provide the best of themselves. Acknowledging that depending on these Angels allows me to find success and fulfillment only makes me more certain that Angel-Mind and the Angels who use it do exist. Without my Angels, I would not be who I am or find myself able to achieve what I do.

Angel-Minds revolve around God's message and Angel-Mind: the individuals who contribute their messages and influence to make society better. Every person on this earth has a message. Each individual leads in their own way; each individual represents one part of God by living and existing. While some reactions or traumas may leave individuals unable to express their needs, Angel-Mind will enable the individual to find the help they need or interpret the action that will allow their contribution of their message. God is represented differently in each one of us, with attributes like leadership or following, spirituality, logical application, or contributing to the joy of others' lives and living. Finding yourself in the role of protector or the one needing protection are all examples of people demonstrating Angel-Mind or of people needing Angel-Mind.

The brain and your individual message are changing as you read this! You may be discovering the puzzle piece of society that your message and experiences are developing into. The brain will continue developing and making refinements until your mid-forties, according to brain scientists.

The present you have to deliver to society is continuing to be wrapped and delivered to humanity, and the wisdom after your mid-forties allows a different application. Each Angel-Mind contributes, cares for one another, protects another, and is in existence to bless humanity. Blessed with logic and spiritual applications, each individual develops different understandings of life.

God is within each expression. Each motivation, desire, and action is because individuals are acting with connection to God-Values or against God-Values. How we choose to survive revolves around the values that God has given each of us and the message inside our soul.

## *The Brain: An Old Model That is Holding Humanity Back*

The brain is a specialized model which hinges its success on survival and changing with the demands of its environment. The brain is ready to change to influence its success and survival. The brain has been resourceful enough to experience success in adapting to dangers and finding safety. Humanity, however, is experiencing bigger challenges than what would be conveyed by surviving a simple predator or prey relationship. The brain needs a [R]evolutionary change to survive. Leadership and protection of individuals, proactivity, and reactivating the ancient programming that was once within God's peoples needs to be awakened. Each individual is still developing and learning to understand God's message, and we each are still learning what to do and how to speak, through how we treat each other.

Just like babies learning, the Angel-Minds within each of us are still learning what to do and how to take care of each other. Difficult conversations about sustainability, protection of vulnerable land areas, and rights of species must be undertaken. Most importantly, we are deciding the next stage of brain development: humans' [R]evolutionary phase: encouraging changes that will reveal Angel-Mind and the saving of the human race.

Evolution and changing of a species to accommodate environmental needs is what gives the feedback of changing into a successful model of survival. Each species that is adapted to its environment will show its success by how it flourishes. Over millions of years, mutations that serve as enhancing adaptiveness (such as the beak design on a bird allowing it better access to food) or being maladaptive to adaptiveness (such as albinism that ruins a species' chance of finding camouflage for hunting or hiding) significantly affected the survival rates of species with different traits. Successful traits reproduced, while unsuccessful traits didn't last over time. The ability to reproduce has been one of the markers of evolutionary success of every species, ingrained in every genetic expression of survival. Genes of particularly successful individuals get passed on, yet genes of individuals that struggled for survival and who did not represent a successful adaptation will eventually die, leading to the stark realization of evolution.

Humans have developed beyond evolution. Communication, supports, and services have allowed each person, regardless of adaptive advantages or genetic hardship, to succeed. But the individuals within society show evolutionary shifts have become less decisive and the search for survival has become less meaningful. The brain, which used to specialize in survival, now faces a more crucial shift, reliance on the decision to activate Angel-Mind and to start the [R] evolution of Angel mind and caring for humanity.

The brain stem is the base of the survival need for humans. It is where the survival instinct has developed, where living and genetic superiority is of utmost importance. Survival reactions are the most important part of the brain stem's function. The selection of natural gifts that enabled survivability caused the human being to develop into one of the most successful creatures on earth. The brain stem provides the motivation on life-sustaining conditions. Survival, respiration, and basic body processes essential to life are handled here. Life or death is so controlling and important, it masks and has hijacked all other thought-processes, from trauma recovery to sharing. The brain stem considers and prioritizes survival fitness of the individual above all else. When operating from the brain stem, Angel-Mind is not a predisposition or even an option. Survival considerations limit thought patterns extending beyond survival. Individuals who feel the stress of acute survival motivations develop a reliable survival trait that allows the brain stem to feel protection or safety. But to achieve Angel-Mind, it is very important to get past the reactionary and urgent set of acute survival motivations and find responsive patterns that interact and contribute to the situation.

The brain stem is focused on individual needs and wants. It is not a team player that allows contribution from each individual; it is entirely focused on self. It has not evolved to take in other needs and ideas. The brain stem limits the thoughts and actions of Angel-Mind. Thinking that originates from the brain stem is reduced to surviving and nothing else. The brain stem must face traumatic experiences, yet because of its survival instinct, it is unable to process the experience. Healing from trauma takes more processing than what the brain stem can do, it needs Angel-Mind processes to work past the damaging and life-threatening process of trauma. Expressions of trauma-thoughts convey living through a traumatic experience and enduring brain changes that negatively affect individuals. Angel-Mind processes restore brain health and individual healing from trauma. Individual potential and Angel-Mind both contribute to make healing from trauma a possibility.

Certain sensory and attention processes are located in the midbrain. The attention and focus that comes from it is integral to understanding where Angel-Mind can impact relationships and taking action. Important to the concept of Angel-Mind and taking action is that many of us don't see things as they are; we see things as we are. This perceptual influence changes the more experiences we have and the more we try to do. Angels need to prioritize self-maintenance and care as goals in their lives so that they can help to take care of others and give them the support they may need.

The forebrain is what separates humanity and animals. It is this and the circuitry within the forebrain that has enabled humanity to have a greater chance than any other species to save itself and this world. The forebrain is actually made of the cerebrum and structures that amount to processing threats, motivations, consciousness and Angel-Mind. It enables individuals to guide themselves and take their place as protectors of the world and of each other, and has been the most recent change in evolution. The forebrain is home to structures like the thalamus, which all sensory information runs through, guiding responses to the information we take in. Below the thalamus is the hypothalamus, which regulates biological drives--feeding, fighting, fleeing, and mating. Each response pattern we feel and inclination that is felt can be attributed to the drive of the hypothalamus and the sensory reception of the thalamus. These drives regulate behavior, and without Angel-Mind to mediate, each human is reduced to a series of drives and instincts that do not represent being the contributor, leader, advocate, and protector God intended.

The cerebrum is made up of two hemispheres, which allow different perspectives. Both hemispheres function differently, enhancing processing and allowing individuals to direct their message. The cerebrum is the most complex part of the brain, responsible for learning, remembering, and thinking.

The cerebrum influences the basic processes of the brain as a sensory organ: sensing threats, taking action, and receiving stimuli. The processing abilities of the brain and its hemispheres allow an interpretation of reality that changes the possibilities of the world and the millions of species that live within it. The cerebrum is made up of two parts: the right and left brain. Angel-flight and being with God is best expressed when using all of the cerebrum, which is one of the most intricate parts of the brain that allows the full range of experiences. These two hemispheres, described as the right brain and left brain, are contained within the cerebrum and can be viewed as the wings that let you take flight.

The right brain develops first and is the center for relationships and creative expression and is how we find ourselves as part of a family. The right brain develops first because it is where spiritual expression and reception are located and begins the relationship with God. Angel-Mind develops from this divine foundation and yearns to continue to protect and help the world and its inhabitants. The right hemisphere is essential for finding meaning in what we do; it is also vital for breakthroughs in using logical applications and how individuals learn what they are good at and what they feel is meaningful. Relationships, spirituality, emotions, and striving for individuality play a role, influencing experiential intake and finding connections and meaning. Interest in others enables empathy or sadness or grieving from the loss of an attachment. The right hemisphere is the silent contributor of processing the environment, seeking safety, paying attention, receiving sensory input, and experiencing the range of emotions that humans feel in life. The right hemisphere is an integral part of expression, which enables a spiritual perspective and subjective view of the whole body of humanity, not just specific or compartmentalized views resulting from logic, scientific methods, or results.

The right hemisphere contains the spiritual portal to God and holds the potential of each individual finding their Angel-Mind and influences relations and connections with everything. Connecting to something spiritually is one of the many gifts from Angel-Mind and influences investment of resources and a feeling of closeness. The yearning, knowledge of, and desire to be in a relationship with God is a right-hemisphere feeling. This yearning for connection to God is integral to expression of the Angel-Mind. Angel-Mind is the highest calling that humanity has been made to achieve and the [R]evolutionary practice that will change humanity. The right hemisphere causes reverence pertaining to the spiritual properties of an environment, thing, animal, or person that needs protection. The right hemisphere contains the perspective and reverence that will heal the earth, protect the many species needing help, and guide humanity toward respect and protection of the earth's inhabitants.

The left hemisphere of the cerebrum is the essence of knowledge and what humanity specializes in. The basis of human society, gathering in groups, harvesting food, building shelters, and establishing a monetary system has allowed humanity to realize the essential aspects of a modern society. Many Angel-Mind advances come from left-hemisphere connections and applications.

The whole aspect of the left hemisphere is logical and compartmentalized. While seemingly at odds with spiritual belief, the connection and engagement resulting from focus and attention from the left hemisphere allows the motivations of sharing, developing, and believing in the message we live with and deliver to complement and contribute to society. Without a spiritual application and connection to a concept with applied logic and directed attention, the world does not make sense. As humans, meaning and reassurance come from the use of logic, which is inspired by the search for connections and understanding. Without the left brain, an individual's quest to understand and participate in life is incomplete. The right and left brain together provide the search for connection, meaning, and understanding of the world and the infinite possibilities of the universe. The left brain applies searching and compiling information, combining with the right hemisphere that adds creativity and spiritual revelations which influences individual identity. Purpose and direction are found through the uniting of both hemispheres. The left hemisphere is about individual focus and attention which influences ability and has allowed humanity to prosper from the learning and application of new information. With each advance and higher quality of living, humanity has prospered and lived better, with a better ability to be each other's Angels.

The ability gained by using logic has resounded within humanity. From different building materials and different farming practices, to different establishments of civilization, the changing methods and enhanced abilities and learning have shown the brain's ability to succeed with changing needs and situations. While the right hemisphere is the silent partner that influences spirituality, creativity, and seizing opportunity, the left hemisphere is the logical, communicative one, communicating and receiving ideas. The left hemisphere also speaks out to constraints and demonstrates all the emotional intelligence and understanding of situations that allow it to succeed and survive within the conditions of the environment.

## *The Window*

The right hemisphere is the hemisphere that allows feelings of family and in-group loyalty to be achieved: creativity, originality, spirituality, and searching for connection and meaning are the offerings from the right hemisphere. An individual is born looking to contribute and relish feelings of acceptance in a relationship, predisposing family connections of loyalty. This draw connects each individual to another, and this right-hemisphere connection also draws people together in relationships. The right hemisphere contains a special brain apparatus, which is the right temporal lobe. It is the special gateway for connection to human spirituality. Angel-Mind is active during the moments of insight or application that connect the gift of the right hemisphere when it merges with the left hemisphere's understanding and application of logic and purpose. Angel-Mind has created inventions and products we use every day without thinking about God in society. These gifts have saved society and improved the quality of life for humans.

The right temporal lobe is the window that allows connection between individual yearning for contribution and acceptance to become unified with God. An individual starts to realize that they are meant to care for, support, protect, and lead others while also revealing their unique greatness when operating with Angel-Mind. Being able to see and celebrate being a leader, finding God, and taking part in the [R]evolution of humanity is the culmination of the Angel-Mind and its development. What does it mean to take part in this [R]evolution that the Angel-Mind offers? It means listening to the needs of the world and its inhabitants, integrating the hemispheres, and taking notice of the state humanity is in and finding how we can contribute. The motivation for connecting with Angel-Mind is the chance to connect with humanity and experience a spiritual atmosphere of giving the best of yourself to everyone around you.

Entering and understanding what it means to bring God in your expression is the key. Connections are being made, connections that have brain-changing relevance. The spirituality that you allow to enter your life in the form of Angel Mind will change your life forever.

## *The Two Hemispheres of Angel-Mind Contributing Unified Meaning*

The hemispheres together represent Angel Mind and connect to God, yet the isolation of a hemisphere from its partner may trouble many. Individuals ask themselves, "What does this life amount to?" or "How can I make any type of progress that I can see?" These are right- and left-hemisphere questions of meaning and compartmentalized focus with feedback—if unanswered, these brain waves can cause a crashing tsunami of destruction. This is the effect of not integrating the brain. The brain has two options for integration: vertical integration, combining the brain stem and its survival motivation with the higher-functioning two hemispheres; and lateral integration, which is combining both hemispheres' abilities so they work as a combined force.

Vertical integration deals with reactionary and knee-jerk responses and changes them into calculated and guided responses. Deep breathing can calm survival responses and encourage deeper thought. Lateral integration concerns the focus on holistic, emotional, and spiritual thinking or sensory reception balanced with compartmentalized and logical thinking. Statements that originate from the right hemisphere may leave individuals feeling overwhelmed: "There is too much that I need to do, I don't have enough time!" The statements from the left hemisphere may scream in protest, "There are so many individuals to visit and to protect! How can I find the feedback that tells me I'm making a difference?" These questions demonstrate the programs that have continually frustrated humans and Angel-Mind: programs of significance. The most significant an individual can become is by relying on their Angel-Mind and living their message they are giving to this world and the individuals within it. Angel-Mind needs no significance; its message resounds with purpose. Each individual is worthy in their existence because of the contribution they give. God has created Angel-Mind to operate without need for merit or evaluation, but with the joy of affiliating with God. Every Angel-Mind is created by God with the programming to do the job it is willing and meant to do: no more and no less. God watches and records, and then builds His next Angel-Mind based on the world's needs. The gifts that one individual with a lower self-esteem may miss are gifts that encouraging Angels, using Angel-Mind, may see and promote. Choosing to exist and continue in the possibility that the contribution of self will come is one of the most difficult and painstaking choices, yet gathering experiences and realizing each moment adds to the development of Angel-Mind and allows celebration and gratitude. Anticipation of the greatness God entrusts each of us with could be considered the longest journey for developing Angels who want to make a difference for others.

Each Angel has a gift, and by relying on and contributing to each other, each Angel delivers their message by doing a job they were specifically designed to heal this earth and save its inhabitants—a stranger whose hand restrains a pedestrian from getting hit by a speeding car at the last second, or someone appearing in a time of crisis for you, responding with reassurance and comfort. Both examples show a protective and supportive aspect of Angel-Mind that returns you to a positive state of mind and existence. Attending a walkathon in support of others in recovery from a disease like cancer, or for those groups who are looking for recognition or equal rights, is Angel-Mind making the difference and demonstrating advocacy and protection on this earth. Angel-Mind can't be rushed, because everything happens in God's time. A frustrating recovery from injury or addiction that might take years to complete is right on time when Angel-Mind understands its own development in the duration. What Angel-Mind does by living life is to contribute and become. Angel-Mind is prolific in its ability to find the right opportunities and to contribute just the right amount of what is needed. Adhering to God's values of contributing our life message by supporting others with leadership, advocacy, and protection, each individual finds the opportunity to discover God within Angel-Mind.

## *Vertical Integration*

The space and performance capabilities between the brain stem and the two hemispheres is an immense storage system of regulatory and sensory equipment. A leap from survival functions, eating and breathing, to discovering your wings and message can be a frightening dive off what is a precarious precipice. Angels who are eager to help and facilitate change may try to fly on their untested wings to uncover a flight path. Angel-Minds often reveal an eagerness to broadcast their message before it is fully developed. This can become frightening and anxious. Angel-Mind is not quite ready to make the contributions it is pointed towards. There is no failure when God synchronizes with Angel-Mind, just connections of success or connections that haven't yet been established. Choosing to be an agent of God and wanting to contribute discoveries and inventions to society with Angel-Mind and God-Values is the success. How long does it take to have the experiences that give wings? The programs that you discover within your individual will tell you. Experiencing anxiety or fear is a signal that you may not be ready to fly. There may be another experience, another attempt, which will prepare you. Only God and Angel-Mind will know for certain. The number of experiences that will guide you to finding meaning and focus are within God's plan.

For those that feel the calling for Angel-Mind or those that shy away from it, both are callings in your soul and reflect the programming that each individual was created and programmed with. Some individuals will jump at the chance to contribute their best self—others will shy away from the possibilities that they hear resounding within them. The cumulative experiences of each individual will predispose traits and ways of operating that allow a stronger individual to rise because of Angel-Mind.

The demands and opportunities that follow and allow a decision like Angel-Mind are a yearning to contribute to God's plan and the gratitude and fitness that keeps the brain healthy. Cardiovascular exercise that allows an optimal amount of brain health while connecting your passions and bringing them to life are essential for encouraging the best flights. Positive thinking is an exercise that encourages the best of society and delivers a level of engaging in solutions that makes the best thoughts rise to meet challenges. Gratitude allows better, higher processing, and more directed thoughts that guide actions and behaviors.

## THE GOD CIRCUIT

The God Circuit is accessing Angel-Mind by looking through the window of the right temporal lobe and then acting to reproduce the action of caring, contribution, and bringing your best self to the situation. Neural pathways are formed in the brain from repeated thoughts, experiences, and behaviors. By continuing to ask and answer your idea of what God has brought you on this earth for, you are reminding yourself of the message God created in you, the message that waits patiently until it is time to express it. You are in the process of knowing and realizing that the message is within your Angel-Mind and patiently accumulating the experiences that make you ready to contribute your message, which will encourage you to find the way to deliver the passions and interests that have guided your message. Continuing the repetition of thoughts, experiences, and actions, all will encourage the journey with God that builds Angel-Mind greatness. The messages we have each depend on the cumulative effect of Angel-Mind; all of society has need of Angels' development and receiving their messages.

The God-Circuit can also be used when feeling a certain resonance with Angel-Mind and God. By bringing my right hand resembling a prayer position against my chest and heart, I achieve a feeling of instant connection by taking spiritual action with God. This strengthens my neural pathways by bringing action with God-Values that contribute to Godly closeness.

Bringing integrative action or ritual into the practice of Angel-Mind, a calming circuit to God is discovered, released, and programmed within. Using Angel-Mind, impulsivity is overcome, greater thoughts are available, and the caring that the entire human race deserves, needs, and will benefit from will finally come to fruition.

There may be times when the energy of God feels like it's so powerfully vibrating within you that can't control it, and there are times of emptiness or loss when you may feel unfilled and find yourself trying to replenish your God-reservoir. These feelings can correlate highly with your expectations. A personal win could mean you are connecting with God and using Angel-Mind, finding the power within yourself to do the most good that you are programmed to do. A feeling of loss, however, can mean that while you didn't win, the path you have taken has inspired a new perspective of working with God through Angel-Mind with your hard work, or the loss has let you or some other Angel-Mind find a more important lesson or idea from the message you have given. Whatever the message you carry, it flows out of you and within you.

But when you feel at your lowest, what can you do? The God-ritual is what I recommend. Whatever you have experienced or are experiencing that is holding you back from touching base with Angel-Mind is halting your message. This is where finding the ritual that brings you happiness, or finding the location of God's resonance and taking that journey, is essential. The rituals that bring happiness and joy show that by connecting to God and following God-Values, each of us is made to be happy. Some individuals exist in God-rituals, trying to maintain happiness and stay away from sadness. Although this is not the highest application of Angel-Mind, accepting the choice of the individual who is in a repeating God-routine is what makes Angel-Mind so accepting and valuable to the human race. When God makes Angel-Mind available, they will use it, but not until then. Allowing every individual the choice of who to be and what to contribute is what makes Angel-Mind advances so important. God-routines can provide a feeling of closeness and comfort by reminding each individual they are with God, and God wants us to be happy. Angel-Mind is ready to feel that closeness and joy, so whenever you need to remember happiness or find comfort, be ready to employ a God-ritual. God-rituals are not just about supporting or reinforcing an individual; they are also about reconnecting an individual to happiness and God.

Maybe it is after a close friend died, or a bad break-up with a partner. Your ritual may be exercising, it may be prayer, or walking in silence in the woods. The God-ritual will help quell the disturbing feelings and will restore the Angel-Mind within. God has made Angel-Minds to be happy so they can take care of themselves and others. The God-ritual will help sustain you so you can be the gift to humanity and serve the many faces of God with Angel-Mind. God and you are partners in success and in Angel-Mind! Finding God with you allows insight into delivering your message. The God-ritual will help sustain you and motivate you.

God and you are partners in helping you find your contribution to humanity. Every step you take is a footstep closer to finding your wings, and that will add to humanity's possibilities and opportunities to gain from your message. It is how we will each protect, serve, and contribute to ourselves and others.

## *Building Faith*

The connection with God and Angel-Mind is demonstrated by everything an individual does and relies on to succeed. The ease with which Angel-Mind makes a connection to God is very consuming. Each moment contains another opportunity that allows Angel-Mind connection to God, which provides personal success. Discovering the heart's yearning for connection with God is feedback that Angel-Mind is waiting. Realizing that each one of us is made to add our own puzzle piece to the greatest jigsaw puzzle of humanity encourages the use of Angel-Mind concepts. Every activity that brings a special application of self encourages faith in self and confidence in the phenomenon of Angel-Mind. Being validated in the purpose you've discovered and being the deliverer of the message you have within, you will consistently gain appreciation and belief, and find faith in how Angel-Mind has made you one of God's many messengers. The faith will continue to stay with you to encourage more applications of Angel-Mind. Every communication will be better than expected because it is you living and hearing the message that God has put inside of you!

Being alone is not lonely, because you are connecting with Angel-Mind, processing at a higher level, and accompanied by the work you are doing for God. Every morning you wake up and enjoy another day to repeat God's message to every one of God's people. There is a purpose in living among the users of Angel-Mind: to support one another, to allow the message of God's love and ability to come from your use, contribution, and reliance on Angel-Mind.

Every day that you connect with possibilities of Angel-Mind, you are building faith that the Angel-Mind within you fits your life and purpose. You will be not only be delivering the message of Angel-Mind, you will be receiving and building the faith that Angel-Mind is a healing and remarkable tool that the human race needs. With the beating of remarkable wings, Angel-Mind can convincingly demonstrate that each mind is meant for higher ground. By continuing to build faith and allow possibility to enter your life with the use of Angel-Mind, the greatest of outcomes can occur.

## "God, Make Me an Angel"

I start every morning repeating the words, "God, make me an Angel." I truthfully believe that is the next step for humanity, so that each one of us can contribute to society, lead others, advocate and support those who need it, and offer protection to everyone. Looking around society, I see the gifts of Angels; every societal advancement has been given by Angel-Mind, a higher state of thinking and a better state of providing for each other. We have been made to find the lost, to reawaken the sleeping, and guide the aimless.

## Present and Accounted for

As one of the users of Angel-Mind, I choose to try to reflect, embrace, and represent what God means to me, and I find contentment in life. Every day I wake up to the possibilities of this wonderful world. I hold myself accountable for what I want to live up to and live for. While accepting that each and every human has the abilities for Angel-Mind, making use of Angel-Mind is more difficult than just accepting the possibility of having society-changing power.

Being calm, limiting distractions, not letting knee-jerk reactions influence decisions, and being as free as possible from anger are the beginning needs of Angel-Mind decisions. Am I getting enough cardiovascular work for my brain health? Am I being grateful and positive enough to allow my best thoughts to affect the situation with encouraging care for others and regard for their specialized message which can help society?

I realize that as an owner of Angel-Mind I have experienced the gifts of many mentors and inventors who have shaped society. I have an awesome respect for each Angel-Mind, which has led to developments that allowed society to become the bulletin board of collective genius.

Some Angels have lost their way. These are the Angel-Minds that have become more reactive than proactive. They are demonstrating a different message than the one God first intended. Traumas, drives from other sources than God, and other experiences and motivations have changed their behavior. Having experienced traumas can slow and change the process of Angel-Mind and cause frustration, but in no way stops the possibilities of Angel-Mind.

Addictions become tools to soothe the soul and may ultimately hamper the development of Angel-Mind. Because of the brain's own striving to find Angel-Mind expression, a frustrated mind does become vulnerable when not achieving the glorious contributing, leading, advocating, and protecting the mind is meant to do.

Finding direction on the path to Angel-Mind can be difficult. The path of true, uncomplicated authenticity can be a source of confusion, because until you started reading this, the assumption is that useful capability is achieved only by working at something. The very nature of the word "work" carries certain connotations and assumptions when it is thought about. Struggling, meeting deadlines, and a haggard existence may be the realization of what a job entails. But with Angel-Mind, instead of working at a job, flying at a job is possible. Contributing and enjoying part of yourself that God has made within you is not work, but a sense of joy. Eagerness at completing God's design brings Angels flying to their job! The flight path for each Angel-Mind is different for each individual, however, and what is frustration for one may be the fuel of development for another. Feeling lost or disoriented for one Angel-Mind may be exactly the feeling of freedom or searching that another Angel-Mind needs to produce its best thoughts. Each individual has an internal motivation and the programs within to find the Angel-Mind it can access. It is just that many of us have forgotten how good it feels to fly. And we all fly in a different way. Some fly to be connected, where others fly to feel individual success and contribute in that way.

Other Angels may have been traumatized and are struggling with forming their own message. The care and support of Angel-Mind will affect the messages, programming, and reality within that is experienced. God is inside each of us, and each of us shares the healing potential of finding the message that will change ourselves and society by contributing it.

God is the border and the boundary. The extent of pain seen in individuals often activates Angel-Mind to want to help when someone is in pain, yet the boundary of the help is in whether the individual, who is hurt, can trust enough to heal. It is with a sense of interdependence that God has made each trauma survivor's healing rely on the relationships that exist between people who have an amount of healing salve for the soul. Each Angel-Mind can heal itself and establish quality relationships that can heal others.

God is present in Angel-Mind; ancient programs were activated to help the human species survive in ancient, forgotten times—programs that were locked into the psyche of humans because the programs amounted to survival in a dangerous world. Providing for survival needs has become less important as Angel-Mind has provided cultural, technological, and agricultural advances and improvements. Reliance on intense focus to survive has dulled. Faulty programs have been adopted, causing ineffective and less-productive Angel behavior. With the loss of focus, Angel-Mind struggles to find meaningful expression. Regardless, Angel-Mind has been the constant in life with God, always developing Angels to grow into better participants in society and influencing progress. Being aware that we are each Angels made to contribute individual gifts and take care of others does allow for an enhanced attitude of participation. Different Angel-Minds heal others with empathy programs, and altruistic ways of volunteering encourage helping those in need; even Angels who practice the Art of Being help those who are seeking something. Expressing and communicating helps individuals to find Angel-Mind by accessing the integrative powers of the two hemispheres. Taking care of others, finding ways to influence the delivery of your unique message, and even being a better human (or Angel, if you are ready to describe yourself that way) is the result of experiencing Angel-Mind.

## AGENCY

Questioning God's involvement in daily life changes when realizing that with Angel-Mind, we are each connected to God. Logic and development of scales and pattern recognition has been able to explain occurrences and make predictions about earthly events. The logic and science of the world have become a study that predicts and explains almost everything except opportunities that Angel-Mind brings and encourages. Predictive ability stops when looking at other Angels who are living amongst us. When God-Values are expressed by a caring question, or a stranger stops to help someone with groceries or when a car breaks down, that is when Angel-Mind is alive. There are so many things that can be explained and understood, yet there are so many things from Angels that arrive unexpectedly by the Grace of God. Those events are the ones that must be listened to and reflected on. Those are the gifts of Angel-Mind that show each of us that God is a sustaining factor of us all. God is connected to everyone, and to all of society.

The predictive nature of the left hemisphere may reveal the inability to make an analysis of God's influence, which may cause frustration. Yet, by living in the present and expressing God-Values as only our Angel-Mind can, we are each made to be the Angels that can take care of each other; we can help each other heal, and we can help our divine nature arise. Or, should I say, we each have the opportunity to. Angel-Mind capability doesn't mean being an automatic Angel. Some individuals operate in a state of emergency, which can limit Angel-Mind capability. Transitioning from the almost hypnotic hold the brain stem's survival motivation has over the brain and finding its path to Angel-Mind, God has put emergency programs within each of us to discover that part of God in our state of highest need. "Emerge and See" programs are when prayer is engaged in and the limiting influence of the brain stem is skipped over to allow Angel-Mind's divine knowledge. The reliance on God to emerge gives confidence and calms the brain, allowing focus and belief. While a feeling of God emerges in the most dire of experiences, Angel-Minds can find themselves skipping over the limitations of the brain stem's survival motivations and find themselves in a state of action by praying and contributing their best efforts to find success in a situation that is unexpected.

It is time for each Angel-Mind to begin the time of Divine Contribution in God's name and essence. Angel-Minds that share God-Values all share Divine Intentions, and the actions they display complement Divine Intervention. Divine Intervention is waiting for God to reveal Himself by saving and protecting others, yet isn't it time for all Angel-Minds to reveal themselves by the protection and support we are made to do by contributing to God's programs and wishes? Divine intentions are the answer to so many of the world's problems.

Experiences in living that cause an individual to rely on bad programming or lack of physical exercise both may hamper God and Angel-Mind. Humans that see God within will be inclined to help others, but individuals that have lost this Angel-sight may not help others because of not viewing behavior from a spiritual window. A one-sided logical or spiritual explanation simply gives feedback that the correct integration of hemispheres will imbue your life with meaning and will bring your life a celebration of the way it is lived. Different situations influence hemisphere use, but logical applications, combined with spiritual and creative meaning, will see everyone with gifts to contribute, as life to protect, and to find and help. Examining Angel-Mind and how it will provide a [R]evolution of humanity is the only way that the human race will survive.

God is alive in each and every one of us. Sometimes indescribable and often unnoticeable except for the Angel-Mind we each use, the supernatural is brought about by works of gifted Angels. Understanding that this gift is given by Angel-Mind is a substantive reason to reintroduce yourself to finding the message that God has programmed in your mind. By choosing to live in this space, you become present with society's needs and wants. You are the contributor to this society, and as a contributor of Angel-Mind, you are an agent of God. God made the correct choice. You are the perfect fit to contribute to this puzzle for humanity's continued survival and what society needs right now.

As society gets bigger, growing with every individual born, the significance of the specialized and individual message within our souls gets lost. As more people come into existence, society becomes less dependent on the messages and gifts within individuals and more dependent on each individual stopping to allow individual praise, appreciation, and gratitude for the gift received. Angel-Mind brings the programs of reinforcement and appreciation for individuals who may be feeling lost. By bringing recognition to others, Angels help establish the entity that remains a mainstay of individual survival.

Protection can be seen as a necessity of living in these times. Protection and safety, while never assured and changed by environmental anomalies, are always best when prayed about. Morehei Ueshiba, an Angel-Mind of peace and defense, first invented Aikido as a martial art that revolved around knowing how and when to use an attacker's momentum against them. His Angel-Mind was working to guide a smaller person against an attacker and was made for those who needed it to protect them and restore peace. A graceful man devoted to peace, harmony, and life energy, Morehei was small in stature and enormously respected. Angel-Mind concepts of awareness, observation, and protection are available to individuals who pray for them, because prayer is God's language, and it will change you. This is just one of the Angels who used Angel-Mind for those who needed protection. Other Angel-Minds offer protection, each Angel lending a hand to any individual who needs it. Knowing that Angels are behind you gives the feeling of protection you may need. Finding a chance to pray for protection allows your mind to seek safety and gives you confidence.

Feeling at peace helps bring an Angel's message to the forefront. Although Morehei probably never realized that his method of protection and peace would allow other Angels' messages to contribute to the world, his message and invention did just that. Not knowing how to protect yourself in a dangerous world can lead to feelings of uncertainty and fear. But just like the self-defense this Angel developed, the trick is in knowing how and when to use an enemy's momentum against them. Angel-Mind and prayer influences calm and better thinking in dangerous situations, which illustrates this Angel-Mind's example of knowing how and when to use the art of prayer to bring protection. God needs you and your message to add to the world. Find the way that you can bring your message life and protect the gift you will give to the world. God made you to add to this world; how will you do it? Find the next integral step of Angel-Mind—living your message.

# LIVING YOUR MESSAGE

## *Finding God--A Choice of Lemons or Limes*

When thinking of a lemon or lime, what reaction is brought about in your body? I'm guessing that your mouth is filled with saliva as a response to the memory of the taste of a lime or lemon. Neurological expectations influence changes in the body as a result of a memory.

The hunger for God is just the same; imagine what the memory of God can do to and for the body and actions of Angel-Mind. Yet the basis of America is secular, logical, and demonstrates a faith in what is logical, what can be observed and predicted. By bringing Angel-Mind to be observed and a predictable part of life is what can save the world and ourselves. Not just volunteering to serve at a homeless shelter during certain holidays, but starting the discussion and taking notice of the disenfranchised peoples and options concerning them. Realizing that Angel-Mind is ready to serve others and bringing it to action is the God-Circuit in action.

Viewing Angel-Mind as a receptive and directive device that encourages and depends on contributions from God-Values and leadership may seem like a daunting task. But it is worthy and will result in Angelhood. The choice of lemons or limes rests on how you want to express God's message within you.

Michelangelo, one of the creators of the artwork in the Sistine chapel, spent years drawing and painting his artwork on the ceiling of the Sistine Chapel, which depicted the story of humanity. Michelangelo's Angel-Mind expressed the artistic message he found within. That message continues to inspire visitors to make plans to see this work of art and take time to reflect on this dedication. Michelangelo's message allows visitors to see and experience the message of God he experienced as a message waiting to be expressed, which he found within himself.

## *The Message Inside*

Humanity's survival fitness has come to be represented only by surviving: Each individual has grown satisfied by a limited number of reactions to satisfy existence. Each individual is choosing to define success by surviving as an individual and not as a group. Every person using Angel-Mind has a special message or instruction for society, one that holds better survival for this earth and humanity. We each hold programming that reveals itself for special abilities and a purpose known only by God.

Angel-Mind is realizing that we have the gift of a message inside of ourselves to offer and contribute to society. Humans are at the highest stage of evolution of our species. Yet, we are not yet taking care of each other or the world as we need to. The [R]evolution of Angel-Mind, while not dealing with any profound physical changes that will enhance survival, does have to do with profound mental changes that will enhance how we care for and lead each other. Accepting the gift that is brought by each individual is a story that illustrates what each Angel needs to attend to, and Angel-Mind begins to accept the privilege of taking care of another and the world.

Agreeing, acknowledging, and resolving that Angel-Mind is the first step to starting our flight with God is when the journey resonates with purpose and meaning. Finding the message within and developing it is a work in progress. When it is selected with attention and delivered to others, it will be encouraging each of us to fly with God too. There may be many messages that resound inside the souls of those who are predisposed towards Angel-Mind, but within all those messages, one will truly connect with society and the culture within it.

Delivering the message is part of Angel-Mind and revolves around cultural acceptance and an individual's message God put in them. Questioning whether a gift is worthy if it is accepted by a million people or just one person who needs it could be a confusing conundrum for someone using Angel-Mind. The reality of living in, directing, and contributing to society is the gift that we each hold! Angel-Mind yearns to contribute and support, thriving with feedback that expresses how it is doing. Appreciation of the ability to live in a society whose advances have been established by Angel-Mind presence is shown by each individual contributing their message they have found within, developing inside of for a lifetime. It develops by attending to the situation and developing personal abilities, passions, and interests. The gift will be ready when Angel-Mind develops and the choice of establishing your unique partnership between God and Angel-Mind arrive at your time. Your Angel-Mind has been begging to contribute to the culture, wanting to find appreciation and acknowledgment for the gifts you give, just as everyone's Angel-Mind does. Appreciation and acknowledgment are the feedback that can act as the wind beneath the Angel-Mind's wings. Protecting and guiding others who are depending on that contribution of Angel-Mind will help you participate in the functioning of society.

Participants in Angel-Mind are referenced throughout this "Living Your Message" section in this book. Angel-Mind and its contributions to society are real. We each must be made aware of how each Angel has contributed to society and how prevalent the concept of Angel-Mind is in society. Angel-Mind and God can lead each Angel, as we can prepare to contribute God-Values to lead others by Angel-Mind. Once we join Angel-Mind's message, the concept of God will unite us.

Cultural receptivity to the message reflects the advances that society is ready to make and the steps it will take to achieve them. Nikola Tesla, a famous inventor, predicted cell phones right after the phone was invented. Yet, the materials and technological steps had not been made yet. Those discoveries rested on the wings of other Angels who had not made their contributions to society yet, which rested on different inventions that would change life. Even though society may move painfully slow for quality-of-life advances, messages of cultural receptivity within each individual may develop separately.

Making the choice to care about this earth and its inhabitants after God has labored and waited over billions of years to create this earth and specialize Angel-Mind to allow humans to be caretakers of earth and its inhabitants is not a responsibility, but an opportunity. God observes and waits. God waits to see if we are the species that can regulate ourselves and create the Heaven that

Angel-Mind is programmed for. Caring for the animals and vegetation on this earth indicates how we are doing with God. Protecting and regulating growth on this planet indicates how Angel-Mind has allowed each individual to achieve supporting God. Taking part in recycling and other conservation practices is what each Angel-Mind contributes and heals with. We've waited long enough to care about our home, others, and to be cared about. Now's the time to start the [R]evolution of this magnificent brain we each have and put Angel-Mind to use to find true caring practices.

Jane Goodall, one of the foremost research experts on chimpanzees and protectors of the species, compiled one of largest bodies of research that had ever been collected on chimpanzees. She loved researching them so much that she would still be out there today, were it not for the stark realization she came to about the chimpanzees' decline in population. In her message of protection, she found it developing in her life experiences and was something she could put to use. When she chose to become a conservationist to protect the chimpanzees' habitat and numbers, her message was revealed.

## *Destiny or Development?*

The question of using Angel-Mind and finding the message, development, and applications within that will contribute to humanity is a question of how we develop Angel-Mind over a lifetime. The brain is in a state of growth and change and is completing refining itself until the middle of our lives. In that time of development, Angel-Mind learns how it will fly and how it will contribute, gaining confidence in each application.

Is each individual who is blessed with the choice of using Angel-Mind destined to change the world? If the society encourages it and starts to realize that humanity's survival is dependent on the valuing each person as a contributor to the well-being of the planet, it can happen. Our destiny will be changed from self-destruction to self-production of answers and solutions to the world's problems. The development of Angels that will set out to contribute and solve the world's problems, as well as a society that is hungry for solutions, will emerge.

There are achievements that have changed society. Each gift has come from an angel. Beethoven's symphonies would never have taken place without his taking note of the music stirring in his soul. His trouble hearing the notes was inconsequential. The Angel-Mind began to work its magic, and the Angel-Mind within Beethoven overcame the hearing that would have silenced his expression of his passion and his gift. As more of the world appreciates the skills and talents that Beethoven's expression of his passion resulted in, Beethoven's wingspan increases as he carries more people and they are encouraged to appreciate musical genius from his contribution. People are carried away by the joy that is brought to those who are moved by his angel-Mind. His destiny to bring the most masterful music to this world was changed not by the challenges he experienced, but by the gift and message that was found within.

## *CLAP Your Hands Together in Prayer*

The true calling of each Angel using Angel-Mind is shown by their application and demonstration of the four basic God-Values of Angel-Mind: contribution, leadership, advocacy, and protection. It is these higher forms of directing thought and action that are the manifestation of Angel-Mind, which contributes to burgeoning minds so they are able to achieve higher processing. It takes an Angel-Mind to realize the benefits of encouraging a mind to find its potential.

By contributing to society, those who are using Angel-Mind are actually taking positions that help others and finding solutions that are needed by this earth. Finding a yearning to fly with and contribute to humanity is definitely an Angel-Mind activity. When Angel-Minds may feel like they don't have anything to contribute, reading and information assimilation can add to Angel-Mind. If information-gathering is not an expression of Angel-Mind that you want to pursue, looking at affiliating with causes and listening to and supporting leaders may be your expression. With contribution, you are giving and earning with your efforts, not taking and spending.

Leadership and guidance of self by finding inner talents is a key toward expression of who you can be. Leaders think differently than those who consider themselves non-leaders. Different priorities, bigger pursuits, and even a range of comfort in difficult situations bless the individuals who choose to be Angels by leading with Angel-Mind.

Leaders blessed with the ability to contribute their own message as well as help others find contribution are the Angel-Minds that find success. Tony Robbins, a life coach who has worked with millions of people, has shown Angel-Mind by helping to support those who want to help others. By turning life strategies into breakthrough results, he shares his message with others and succeeds. He contributes to others' success by showing them just how high they can fly.

Clapping your hands together in prayer is an integration exercise that involves both hemispheres. God has always wanted us to operate from Angel-Mind and to communicate with Her. Find the possibilities of Angel-Mind by your rapport with God and by using the God-circuit you plant by taking action with your thoughts.

## *Seeking Spirit*

The spirit we find inside of ourselves is how the programs within us are delivered. This powerful realization of how we operate and deliver the messages within us will determine comfort, expression, and belief in yourself and your contribution. The acceptance of what you contribute and who accepts it will be an indicator of how much Angel-Mind society is operating with.

The greatest of personalities have understood the necessities of delivery and the mass appeal that their talents have brought them. Oprah Winfrey operates with a sense of Angel Mind that is her message. It is her own personal spirit that makes her the presenter and publicity magnet that she is.

Her spirit resonates with how people want to feel today. Other Angel-Minds resonate with you and are probably whom you're thinking of right now.

Ellen DeGeneres is a hugely popular talk show host who appeals to audiences in a different way: by using her skills as a comedian. Appealing to audiences with a type of happiness that others cannot duplicate, her spirit presentation makes her an unforgettable presenter whom people want to see.

Comedians, talk-show hosts, and presenters each have been able to find their own spirit which has made them a success at what they do. Ask yourself where you've been successful, and I'm guessing it's because of your spirit that has affected the programs you are running and delivering.

Society is changing with the amount of spirit that is finally being accepted. The brain's thalamus and hypothalamus intake different stimuli, telling individuals who they are and what orientation they are. Spirit-orientation can be seen by the large amount of diversity being demonstrated and accepted. No longer are individuals having to hide their true identity. Guided by the spirit within the individual, people are now feeling the freedom to live as who they truly are. Angel-Minds are accepting of what society is giving and encouraging self-acceptance. Congratulations to the individuals with the acceptance of their spirit-orientation and the Angel-Minds that have supported and advocated for them. And thanks to the Angel-Minds that have accepted these spirit-orientations and encouraged acceptance. A television show called *I Am Jazz* is a show about a transgender teenager who has been given enough support and allowed to develop such a strong voice that "coming out," was a natural choice. With Angel-Mind and spirit orientation, it's not "coming out," it's "flying out."

Different drives and intentions also affect Angel-Mind flight and the spirit in how life is approached. Despite a male standard and prototype of achievement in business, feminism has shown that women can achieve and display as many or more traits of success as males can. Contributing to God's faces with Angel-Mind allows role models to be established of a different type of success. Sheryl Sandberg's Angel-Mind allowed herself to see a different reflection of success and ability when she wrote her book *Lean In*. It shows the connections she sees with women, leadership, and working successfully.

Another example of Angel-Mind would be the extraordinary storytelling of J.K. Rowling. Her creative stories tell of the adventures of Harry Potter, a hero that existed in a magical world. Angel-Mind allowed her to write with such passion that her stories gained worldwide acclaim.

## *Experiencing and Expressions of Angel-Message*

Experiences and expectations of the brain's perceptions can affect behavior of Angel-Mind. Even operating as a protector and caretaker for humanity, misguided and misplaced assumptions can mean differing outcomes for a message from Angel-Mind. The individual programs and messages we each run through Angel-Mind combine with the experiences we have or are having and can alter Angel-behavior. This is very important to how each individual's message manifests and is expressed.

While the culmination of personality, experiences, and bringing the highest of thinking is important to the expression of Angel-Mind, it is also important to find how to express it. As humans, the programs we run often lead to similar destinations. Studies of people using location devices show the repetition of similar patterns again and again. The same supermarket is visited, the same gas station is filled up at. Attempts to provide consistency may reflect a routine that is bringing exactly what your brain and expectations need. This is a different part of God-routine, a schedule of activities that encourages fulfilling personal needs and happiness requirements each person has, which need to be satisfied for a satisfying experience. Different experiences may result in running different programs. Programs stressing rushing or efficiency may cause individuals to make mistakes by pushing themselves to achieve too much. Programs of superiority may cause bullying. Yet the same programs can cause striving for best self in another individual, in a different application. Some of the most evident programs in society today are programs of disconnection, which can lead to atheist beliefs, or programs of individuality demonstrated in various methods of operation. Vulnerability from isolation leaves others to not feel protected or wanting to protect others. Straining for survival may highlight the reactionary, knee-jerk thinking which illustrates feelings of not being able to need or depend on others that can disrupt the process of integration.

Can you think of any programs being run by someone in your life right now? Finding the commonalities and needs each of us have within, and being able to help others, is one of the Angel-Mind programs which helps individuals to the same locations that everyone strives for. Protective and isolationist programs that are run may show how the individual has been hurt by not achieving group acceptance and is trying to protect from the hurt of exclusion.

Although that can be initially how programs are started, the gift of Angel-Mind is a counterpoint to isolation from others. It is an interactive and changing routine of goals, connecting with others, and finding contribution to society. Angel-Mind is more than finding a God-routine of certain locations or items that will keep someone happy. Happiness is God's promise to his Angels, that we each can be happy and content by using God-Values and satisfying programs within. Angel-Mind is ready for so much more than routines of comfort. Happiness is within, and the extraordinary can be achieved by stepping outside routines of happiness and risking contribution to others. Failure can occur when risking by stepping outside the boundaries of safety. But outrageous success can be the reward. Inventors don't know that their inventions will work; sometimes it takes a spill to release the supernatural achievements of Angel-Mind. Battery acid being spilled demonstrated Alexander Graham Bell's invention of the telephone. His discovery of the usefulness of the telephone came only after his spilling battery acid on himself and his need to call his house for help.

Other spills may involve a search for deeper meaning and possibilities for a different calling. An "accident" may be your calling to find an undiscovered potential or existence and to examine why you are here. Accidents or uncharacteristic incidents that occur can cause attention to factors of life and existence that bring Angel-calling. It is a special moment when acknowledging the idea that your life and survival is precious because God needs your message! That Angel-calling is available to each individual using Angel-Mind. Live for God. Bring His message and world to manifestation! Because He planned on, needs and wants, even relies on, your contribution.

Each individual is so important in that if we all use our Angel-Minds and ability we will fulfill His plans. Life reveals God's plans, and Angels discover ways to complete them with their abilities and gifts; living will see them come to fruition. Living is the process of discovering the gifts and message and revealing it to complete God's plans. You decide whether you bring your wings into existence with Angel-Mind, making your message that God needs so much more affecting and vibrant when you use it. Angel-Mind lifts those who need to speak their message to a better location. It is a miracle to observe others' messages that take place and add to God's plan without the individual yet having accessed Angel-Mind or having acknowledged accessing it. Looking at individuals who are blessed with the highest of skills will often bring admiration of the message they are delivering for God without even being aware of it! How important those individuals are!

Malala Yousafzai, a girl in Pakistan, was shot in the head by the Taliban after speaking out for education rights for girls. She survived, and her message grew even stronger when she became the youngest recipient of the Nobel Peace Prize. Leading the discussion about rights for education and showing the resolve that motivates all leaders, her being shot by the terrorist group made her burgeoning message of education as a right for girls to find its place in mainstream society. What could have been regarded as an accident that would have silenced her message of leadership and education for girls was the pulpit that this Angel flew to speak from. Her Angel-Mind survival and motivation spurred awareness of her message far more than any individual pursuit to educate the world about females' rights to an education.

## *Finding a Pathway to Becoming*

Programs that can be struggled with but are not limited to are: programs of significance, simplicity programs (because no human operation or relation is just a simple matter without consequences or drawbacks), intimacy and sexuality programs, self-worth programs, programs of conflict or struggle, impulsivity programs, or distraction programs. Do you find any of these programs causing difficulties in your life? Some of these programs may interfere with how we see God. Approaching satisfaction of the programs within from acceptance is the true way to stop struggling with them. Acceptance of the internal programming that God planned for us can signal a continual challenge, which Angel-Mind will struggle with to find a purpose for. God put that program in us for a reason. Discovering that reason may be impossible, but accepting the program is within is a substantial victory. Accepting that the program is within and may be causing discord can be the step God needs you to make so you can start your flight of accepting the Angel within.

Dictators have come to power through abuses of ideas that have allowed them to convince others to deny God-Values because following their leadership is the only way to exist. Unfortunately, it's not leadership when dictators lead. It's ownership of faulty programs that allows them to suppress the glory and joy which occurs when Angel-Mind manifests. Dictators who rule with terror and violence never receive the gifts of Angel-Minds that they could use and profit from. Angel-Minds are never free to contribute their unifying message of God within them.

One of the most beautiful expressions of an Angel-Mind was conveyed by Harriet Tubman, the famous and revered leader of The Underground Railroad. She transported many slaves to freedom and found her message in the care and protection she supplied to others. Finding leadership within her programming routines, she found that she could contribute by freeing slaves and not losing one in the process. Angel-Mind developed within Harriet's programs and showed the world what true leadership is about. She continued her life and development of Angel-Mind by taking care of those she freed who came to rely on her for support.

## *The Destiny of Angel-Mind*

All behavior reflects the search for a God-experience, or something that brings what Angel-Mind offers each of us: contribution, leadership, advocacy, and protection. Even though we each may have the undiscovered abilities we search for, it doesn't mean that we are aware of them until they are developed within us. A passion for dance which lends our life a new rhythm, or a new-found understanding of a subject researched can enhance understanding and formulating action for a topic that needs attention. Angel-Mind assimilates and is ready to process new information before we realize it is available. The destiny of Angel-Mind, however, rests on the community that makes up the support and contribution, leadership and protection. Angel-Mind experiences individuals take part in are to discover the God-experience and to uncover God-Values. Every Angel understands that while it is important to develop Angel-Mind as much as possible, Angels rely on following other Angel-Minds to achieve the successes that will eclipse previous standards with new abilities and achievements. That is God's plan. Angels with different skills are needed to provide for a more diverse populace. As Angel-Mind arises as a societal factor, every individual has that yearning, and the behaviors and achievements demonstrated reflect the ideas of satisfying the needs of the world as each individual takes their place as an Angel who will contribute to the human race. The goal of every Angel-Mind, however, is not to surpass previous Angel-Minds. It is to contribute.

## GOD'S REFLECTION

The interpretations of the situations and the present that faces each of us is in will be different for all and can determine behavior depending on which hemisphere individuals are looking out of. The myriad possibilities which God represents can be expressed by the millions of stars winking as you look out in the night sky and see the unorganized brilliance of space. God is the opportunity each individual has, and the joyous celebration you feel when finally deciding to become the Angel you have always been made to be. How you choose to make Angel-Mind contribute to the situation is how we each exist with God and how God-Values have moved us to be. Each moment is an epiphany of realizing the message you have found within, looking through the windows which we see God's reflection and deliver that message.

Think of how many times you have looked at something and your soul has soared. The Golden Gate Bridge in its magnificence, being in a wilderness refuge and staring with jaw agape because there is nothing so beautiful as nature in its uninterrupted form and chaotic synchronicity. Each creature knowing exactly what it has to do and achieve to exist.

Each of the Angel-Mind's hemisphere specializations determines what we will see and the path that will be followed to achieve God's message within. Finding the Angel-Motivation that contradicts social norms, expresses individual understandings, creativity, and passion is exactly what Angel-Mind needs to do! The biggest blessing is to be a contradiction to what might be considered expected! Passions run deep and true, and for Angel-Mind, there is nothing quite as convincing or as inspiring to Angel-Mind as passion. It brings the biggest brain changes and carries the most motivation to follow it.

Belonging to self is the biggest reflection of Angel-Mind and is truly what God intended for each of us. Finding the excellence within your existence by doing what you love is soul-nurturing for Angel-Mind. Finding reliance on the brain's ability to produce answers in novel or unlikely situations is exactly what it is designed for.

Suze Orman's Angel-Mind spirit-programming and passion has encouraged her to become a motivational author and financial advisor who understands and thrives on numbers and math. A vice president in an investment company, Suze found her message was needed by anyone who struggled with numbers and finances. Writing several books and being a presenter of her own TV show, she won a Gracie Award for Outstanding Program Host. Her message was demonstrated with such excellence that she found her wings. Being good at numbers reflected how Suze's Soul Work with financial aspects affected her Angel-Mind and motivation to learn and demonstrate a captivating message. Tossing stereotypes aside, Suze found her achievement in numbers and finances, what might be considered a stereotypically male profession. Her Spirit-Programming made her understand numbers and the basis of finances.

## *Revolution Angel-Mind*

Success is the revolution that Angel-Mind is made to achieve with the best thoughts and highest motivations. Angels protect and support humanity because Angel-Mind has heard God's message of protection. Sharing similar messages that all originate from God and result from dealing with the world, society's dependence on Angels needs to be acknowledged and understood. God's message of togetherness is the calling that Angel-Mind understands and contributes to. Angel-Minds have found a message of God's caring and influence. The [R]evolution of humanity is coming, and for those of us who are keenly aware we are constructing the thoughts, prayers, and awareness to facilitate the movement.

Human progress and learning continue to rest on the wings of Angels. In a society where "fitting in" has become overvalued, new solutions and different approaches are so unrecognized but needed. Diversity and acceptance of that diversity is what Angel-Minds specialize in and what society needs. Creators, inventors, and scientists have been influencing and stirring how God wants each individual to live and make use of because of Angel-Mind. Angel-growth and specialty are manifested from Angel-Minds supporting beginning Angel-Minds in what they do and realizing that their job that God gave them is to contribute their best selves. Each person is blessed with a brain that is uniquely different from everyone else's, and part of the blessing is being able to reveal what God made their Angel-Mind to be.

But while human communication has let each human profit from another human's expertise, the isolation of humans from God's message, protection, and love has not enhanced society. Angel-Mind is set to change that, once individuals accept God's calling. Society's tipping point is here. Angel-Minds' use and encouraging support needs to start to define and revolutionize society. Giving back, finding new solutions, and being aware of possibility needs to become a priority.

Overpopulation, climate change, wildlife displacement, and food growth techniques serving the population all indicate planet health and show how unprepared humanity is to meet challenges that are manifesting today, leaving humanity exposed to extinction. Overexpansion is leading species that need to be preserved as a function of global health to die. Revolution Angel-Mind is not just an uprising; it is where Angel-Mind takes flight to lift Humanity to better living.

## *Angel-Minds Revealing Themselves*

A [R]evolution in humanity is not impossible or improbable. Yet we must choose it to make it happen. By relying on each individual that is on this earth as a potential contributor to help humanity survive, we may just have a chance. Each individual is worthy of the responsibility of saving God's creations. In fact, the success the world is finding is a direct indicator of reflecting God's values and success with existing.

Angel-Mind needs to become a new standard. Humans who have used Angel-Mind have brought humanity and its advancements to where they are currently, yet the earth and its inhabitants still have many more improvements to be made. God has many faces, and we each bring ourselves that much closer to representing God when revealing Angel-Mind. The reflection of God is shown in each of our faces.

## *God Is an Individual Gift*

God is within the discovery of each individual and allows connection to each sequence and happening of our lives. This allows humans to demonstrate goodwill and balance or evil and faltering inconsistency. Individuals are much more likely to end up relying on and demonstrating Angel-Mind's highest mental capacities than performing and living how they are told to act, which is why this book is not a book of laws, but instead a book demonstrating examples and flight plans. Boundaries, laws, and limits are made to be broken: reaching excellence is a boundary of satisfaction and quells the tendency to overstep. Humanity has always reached higher with Angel-Mind, always finding achievement with angel-Mind and God. Excellence and goodness are not something that needs to be regulated in God's plan but is to be provided in Angel-Mind and God's connection. The individual interpretation of God-Values that are programmed directly into Angel-Minds allows individuals to demonstrate meaningful God-Values of contribution, leadership, advocacy, and protection.

These God-Values are achieved by Angel-Mind in an amazingly complex demonstration of faith and belief. These standards expressed within Angel-Mind all will save the human race, because the goodness of humans operating with God's message is undeniable. And the goodness will moderate the evil that is expressed by others in this world that have not yet found Angel-Mind.

Each individual is a participant in choosing action that reflects God's exact timing. Each individual will choose to act on or conceal the programming that we each have been created with. This encourages dependence on other Angels, and allows other individuals dependence on Angel-Mind capability. Synchronicity with Angel-Mind contribution is rewarding and encourages the best outcomes. A decision must be made to engage in living the life, responsibilities, and opportunities that come with being an Angel and when to participate and support a society that resonates with God-Values.

## *Soul (Sole) Work*

Passions contribute to and lead the advances of Angel-Mind. Individual work that demonstrates passion and involvement of the mind contribute to the soul and enhance individual abilities. The ability to choose to use Angel-Mind and invest self in connecting and contributing to the human race brings community, happiness, and hopefulness. Angel-Mind is created just for that purpose. The journey we take with God and the contributions we try to make in society according to messages found within our soul can be very rewarding and healing. Humans are made to work with others, yet the real advances will come from the decision to use Angel-Mind and find reward in working individually. We are each made to contribute to the common good with individual messages of doing what stirs our soul, from developing and inventing to choosing to follow other Angel-Minds. Conflicting messages in group settings may feel polarizing for the God-Value of contribution. Yet each human is made to contribute their message from God, for each of us has to live well. Individuals who contribute their best work can find their passions while living, developing interests, and demonstrating commitments to values. Leadership is a byproduct of passion, interest, and engagement. The ability for individual work contributing to the changing face of God is representative of how engagement in an activity can change each individual by the power of choosing to focus and activate Angel-Mind.

The brain and mind change and specialize as work and life are participated in. The Angel-Mind is able to specialize in the work it does and succeed with specialization in that work. Using motivations of supporting others and contribution as key motivations, Angel-Mind is able to be an adept learner. Delivering the message you hold in yourself is when you will be happiest; working to construct it, finding it, and revealing it will be the moments you really are alive. The work you're motivated to do by yourself is the work and interests that reveal themselves as you connect with what your soul is made to do. The truth of your soul's contribution is revealed by your interests and motivations you work at and feel rewarded by engaging in.

## The World Waiting to Receive

For many, the make or break of society has already left their soul wanting more. They have not experienced enough support to encourage Angel-Mind Proficiency, and there are definite needs that are being expressed which may run counter to the time and journey it may take to realize your message within. Inside each Angel-Mind, there is an instinctive knowledge that the world and its inhabitants deserve better. There may need to be more time allowed for each Angel-Mind to develop a message that will contribute to the world with love, insight, and compassion. Society is not protecting or supporting the world's occupants, not letting them discover their messages or live God-Values. But realizing these constraints and encouraging the influence of Angel-Mind, the world is improved. Individuals may find discontent with their system that seems to be at odds of prosperous growth and healing. Contribution and advocacy for each other is a healing factor that allows contributing to another's message that may have lost vigor and purpose.

Think about the healing that occurs when feeling accepted, empowered, and made to feel worthy. In the human condition, debt, deficit, and longing become quicksand that swallows an individual up, taking away happiness, security, a person's faith in themselves, even their identity. Debt usually becomes the default style of judgement. It becomes easier to say that an individual can't do something than finding them the support to allow them to succeed. But individuals who contribute their presence and God-Values to others actually give the gift of healing that infuses confidence in being able to achieve something. Contributing reassurance, companionship, and acknowledgment can be a very big part of an Angel's message.

### THE MESSAGE SENT AND A RESPONSE IS GUARANTEED

Deciding to live the message you find inside of you offers you definite forms of feedback. How your feelings and responses change when you become comfortable sending your message out to the world! Are you living your joy by accessing Angel-Mind? Those around you will see the change when you are exuding your leadership and contribution! The God-Values that Angel-Mind inspires will cause you to be a center of action because you realize how much you can contribute your own skills and self to. And it is not because you're looking for the attention, it is because people see who you are, and they know that anyone who resounds with Angel-Mind and God so clearly is demonstrating leadership worth following.

When the message is sent with the God-Values of contribution, leadership, advocacy, and protection, there will be feedback in how something has changed, both how you look at yourself and how others look at you. Your Angel-Mind will be emerging, giving you the chance to carry others to spots they never dreamed of going but knew they always wanted to go. With the Leadership that is so reflective of the individual message, programming, and abilities within, you will achieve new heights at how you relate to others and how they relate to you.

Friends and strangers will start noticing changes in you because of Angel-Mind. They will be sharing that zeal for God that you are sharing with them! Because it is a gift when you can look at your friends and be grateful that you are sharing your time and gifts with them and they are grateful for your contribution. The contributions will add to both your experiences, the leadership will let each of you excel, and the support you give to the person by believing in their interests will enhance their sense of self. That protects their humanity and will encourage their flight with Angel-Mind.

### RIGHT MESSAGE, RIGHT TIME

Messages fit each individual precisely, resembling the uniqueness of the human brain corresponding to its function. Each message that finds its place is a message correlating to the right time and place. Angel-Mind may see the opportunity for many changes that will improve society, but society may not be ready. The right time for a message from Angel-Mind may seem like right now, but the right time also deals with societal consciousness, acceptance, and focus.

While the message may not find its place when it originates, the concepts of Angels advancing the success of Angel-Mind by using God-Values of contribution, leadership, advocacy, and protection makes all things possible. These values will never lose their application or importance; their application will influence the development of a message that matches the times. God waits for society to adopt His values and His ways. But society can be slow to respond and resistant to Angel-Mind ideas and behaviors. Individuals are doubtful of the power that comes from adopting God-Values and using Angel-Mind. Individuals are not fully realizing the power of Angel-Mind by never harnessing the remarkable power of God's messages.

### *No Death—Angel-Mind Lives on With Effort, Protection, and Advocacy*

Have you ever wondered where the energy and investment goes when you are working to emulate God-Values? After the work is done, the invention is made, or the God-Values change someone's life, the energy just doesn't stop. The energy continues on in a different form. Whatever the application of Angel-Mind changed, improved on, or contributed to, your energy never dies. A person you worked with on understanding learning concepts or spent weekends with enjoying activities exists with Angel-Mind energy. Even a bit of weeding you did as a renovation project to help clean up an abandoned lot—your energy remains in that location and action used to restore the location. The weeds get replaced by roses, the roses get picked by an individual interested in wooing another, and your Angel exists in that smile as the flowers are received. Every aspect of the world is driven by energy, and because of that, many of the Angels who first changed this world are still here when they are remembered.

There is no proof of nonexistence when an individual investing in God-Values dies. But there is proof of existence and of a change in the recipient who received the attention from the Angel-Mind. There are those individuals who have been changed by Angel-Mind who are energized when they remember them in their nightly thanks, gratitude, and prayers that keep those Angels alive. The things that received the energy change and are showing the influence of Angel-Mind, because of the energy contributed and given. The actions of protection and support will be some of the most rewarding energies ever given. There is nothing more rewarding as reinforcing the God-Values with Angel-Mind actions and decisions. Support and protection are how the earth and God depend on Angel-Mind to survive and prosper.

# The Flight

## *Self-Regulation Is the Key to Experience God's Message and Understand It*

The journey of each individual is to discover the kinship we each have with God and the message that the journey with God has shown us. Important in this relationship is the self-regulation that each of us has to live that message and see it develop. Many messages that Angel-Mind has for society may take time to develop and extend past immediate gratification or rewards that offer feedback. Being able to use Angel-Mind is the reward; working for God is the prize.

## *Individual and God-Given Greatness*

There are people that seem to be predestined leaders, people who take their group's achievements and abilities to a higher level. Some individuals are so predisposed towards individual achievement that they have difficulty working in team situations. But it is their excellence in the jobs they do and the greatness they achieve that makes their performance speak so loudly that they are known by many, and some might say they are even blessed by their abilities. Other leaders easily manage group work and communicating with others easily. An individual's predisposition to use either or both hemispheres, their brain structure, and their being an individual affects the unique message they deliver. By being so individual and dedicated to their work, their performance has allowed them to be known by all. Soul work has let them discover their passion, and they have flourished.

Steve Jobs of Apple Computers, or Kurt Cobain from the Seattle Grunge band Nirvana, are both examples of individuals with exceptional talent who may not have been prepared for the success they were offered by society. Jobs was reported to have difficulties operating with individuals who worked for him; Cobain had difficulty accepting the adulation from screaming fans that followed him. Both individuals are popular and well-known examples of Angel-Mind taking individual success to a new level which affected everyone in modern times.

While it may be easy to imagine contribution, the flight of an Angel using Angel-Mind will never be easy—just possible. If you choose to look with an idea of bringing God-Values to fruition and appreciate with gratitude, you will find the wind beneath your wings. Some of the greatest Angel-Minds are so developed that allowing them to lead and choosing to follow them can be a valuable choice of expressing your message.

The feelings of apprehension you may feel when examining leadership possibilities of Angel-Mind may steal the wind from your wings. The gift and message you have carried within your soul since birth may have changed in cultural relevance. Once, you imagined your message affecting all of humanity; now, only a few people will listen to your message, let alone act on it. The gift of Angel-Mind continues in society, regardless of cultural acceptance. The gift of your message is the gift that God has given you. All types of gifts bring joy to all types of people, but the gift you have been given is a gift to be celebrated, because it has been made just for you! Regardless of whether you see your message contributing to others or searching for what to contribute, know that as a representative of God by using Angel-Mind and continuing to adhere to Angel-Mind principles and God-Values, you are changing the world for the better.

## *Angel-Mind for the Times*

Technology rewires the brain every time it is used. Attention spans get shorter, the sense of hurry that society experiences becomes more pressing as answers come to the brain faster and faster. The mind starts to work against itself; the message of the individual continues to be obscured. Individual and concentrated focus works against the need for holistic views of health. People need the uniting force of God. The universality of God and Angel-Mind is reinforced by reliance that is shown by using an invention or societal breakthrough. Everyone benefits from individuals that have chosen to contribute their message to society when they walk with God and express and appreciate Angel-Mind. As Angels, we each depend on and are influenced by the realization that God is with us when Angel-Mind is expressed. A combining force unites all who are reliant on the advances that have come from Angel-Mind and who realize God is within.

## *Angel Mind Crying Out Loud*

Each of our souls has a need to support and accept others, to be with them. Each individual is meant to be present with another. Brains are made to do that with their unique hemisphere applications, and if we follow Angel-Mind, we can represent God and support the people within society. There is no need for cell phones, no need to live in an illusion of constant connection, because Angel-Mind is that connection. Angel-Mind is being motivated to connect and protect society by realizing the holistic nature of being with God, rather than being drawn away from God and society by relying on individuality to survive. Angel-Mind wants to contribute and be part of, to join society and be part of who we were made to be.

The connection to God through Angel-Mind is quite powerful: contribution, advocacy, protection, and leadership can overwhelm an individual and distract them by reintroducing God's values they have been longing for into their psyche and being. The God-Values of contributing, leadership, advocacy, and protection return our wings to us. Those values within us help reconnect individuals to encourage sharing, cooperating, and contributing to society. Altruism returns as Angels fly up to help, because helping others results in resounding harmony with God. That contribution can give the acknowledgement and feedback that is so important to Angel-Mind so it realizes it is interacting with the environment and revealing God's message. Healing hands rebuild dreams, strong backs help carry the weight of burdens too big for one individual. Sharing workloads that overload one individual makes a job welcoming for a group of individuals ready to put the time in. Protecting vulnerable groups becomes joyful because their voices are finally heard and they can be listened to, encouraging Angel-Minds to accept and acknowledge the necessity of supporting vital issues and topics of concern relating to the affected group.

Being part of society is a series of activities that Angel-Mind connects with. Programs that Angel-Mind is running are essential to providing and receiving caring from society. Angel-Mind is being distracted by the experience of a multitude of novel societal activities that change the brain's appetite for individual focus at an amazing speed—so fast, it may seem that this "multitasking" can achieve everything it is supposed to be able to.

Individual focus and brain specialization uses directed focus that was made for survival in the early world. One task at a time, emphasizing and prioritizing survival activities first was how the brain and expectations were made to work. Earlier in humankind's development, true Angel-Mind's multiple applications came from motivations, passions, and gifts from within.

The brain cannot discern between attentional neurotransmitters that apply to novelty or an actual threat to survival. The brain cannot tell how much energy it needs to expel and put forth for survival when a chat window opens on your computer monitor, or if your attention is ripped away by the roar of a lion from your visit to the zoo. Angel-Mind gets lost in the appeals of marketing and other draws. Attentional focus which once allowed survival in a dangerous environment now survives in a world of beeps and squawks, each representing a distraction which impedes Angel-Mind, and is part of the reason why technology is so addictive to humanity. All of the same brain appeals used to survive back then are now being used to influence the brain to react in a mode of survival.

## *Addictions*

Addictions are the distractions which can be a telling sign that people are not happy. Life has become so overwhelming that rather than helping and contributing to society, a fake feeling of freedom is invested in. Brought on by a substance or behavior that changes the experience of an individual, this mind-numbing substance ruins Angel-potential. Rather than engaging in humanity, disconnecting from humanity is what the addictive substances cause. Addiction can happen for many reasons. It can be that challenge that is a result of a personality trait, or a hunger that is just being discovered because of inability to process life situations. All Angels have challenges, yet all Angels have gifts to overcome those challenges, too

Reconnecting with society and getting involved, helping or volunteering can be the biggest source of healing sustenance to fight addiction for an Angel-Mind. The biggest changes happen when supporting, leading, and immersing an individual struggling with addiction into humanity and leadership principles. Companionship is a worthy tool; the individual may have felt alone for too long. Every Angel can enjoy and share the companionship of each other. If you haven't discovered your programs that invite you to help or be with others or you are finding programming that is dissuading you from being with and helping others, let me encourage you to think about them now and find what is true.

## *Discovering the Inner Angel*

The drive and the passion that Angelhood unveils will awaken the resolve of Angel-Minds everywhere to help. Angel-Minds are waiting to contribute what their inner Angel knows and has been developing ever since God created Angel-Mind. Every development that has arisen to make life better has come from Angel-Mind, a need to make living better and easier for all. If hesitancy is felt, the Angel-Mind is not ready to serve yet! It needs to learn to protect itself from trying to do too much. There are other Angel-Minds ready to share the message of God's love, connection, and caring with everyone. It is through this window of Angelhood that God is viewed, which opens the possibility that no matter who we are, no matter what circumstances we come from, we do have a duty to contribute the best of ourselves.

When did becoming an Angel start to be trivialized? It is truly one of the most resounding and determined decisions an individual can make. Acting and aligning with God-Values that restore humanity and infuse behaviors with directed purpose, the possibilities that are seen through a spiritual connection can demonstrate how we will add to the world with our message that resounds deeply inside each of us. Throughout life, different messages and developments will be refined within us. Some angels struggle with challenges that may prevent them from seeing their ability or gift. But the truth is always that each Angel who has that challenge also has a gift to overcome that challenge. It is so important to understand the interplay and interaction between the many challenges faced and experienced. There are so many challenges today, yet there are so many opportunities to use Angel-Mind and to become the Angel the world and its inhabitants need. The circumstances before humanity seem overwhelming.

The Earth is needing an Angel's touch. Humanity needs the accompaniment of God's guidance and companionship. Change needs to come from Angels' contribution, leadership, advocacy, and protection so that living well and surviving well can belong in the same sentence.

Surviving in a world that hasn't acclimated to the demands so many people on earth are making is what is causing disruptions in the world. Survival programs are causing erratic behavior and interfering with how humans are relating to each other. Demonstrating Angel-Mind becomes difficult and almost impossible for many operating from the perspective of survival-mode. Humans' ability to access Angel-Mind weren't designed for such stresses, and hesitancy to reveal and use God's emergency programs that rely on prayer further complicates things. Angel-Mind cooperates and contributes to each other except when it hasn't integrated in its hemispheres which encourage Angel-Mind behavior. But even taking all this into account, I smile. I know that we have an advantage. Each angel, no matter the challenge, has a special gift in themselves. It is waiting to connect with Angel-Mind, to be let out and released to help others. We just need to work together, relying on the God we have, between each of us and the advances that Angel-Mind has brought to society, each individual has access to the healing power of Angel-Mind.

The gift is the passion that consumes us. Angel-Mind may not announce the gift as early as when it first ignites, but it will save the entire human race when we decide to use it together as Angels in Arms, when our wings are folded together in the goodness of what we can do.

Jonas Salk, inventor of the polio vaccine, was once asked if there might be a reward that could be offered to him for developing the vaccine that prevented the childhood disease of polio. He declined the offer, mentioning that it was the people's vaccine. Salk's discovery of the vaccine was the reward of his Angel-Mind ability manifesting into a solution. His passion sated, Salk was able to receive the fulfillment of the message that started within. The sole work he had devoted himself to was so rewarding and fulfilling so that he had achieved soul fulfillment.

No payment was necessary. The gift of Angel-Mind combining with passion became the wind beneath this Angel's wings and was the satisfaction from achieving a solution for humanity's struggle. Finding that message within is one of the most satisfying parts of being human and using Angel-Mind. His gift was delivering the message that was within him. It had been developing as his interests grew and changed. As he continued to offer the message which changed humanity with the advancements he made, he discovered the wings that come with using Angel-Mind.

While many Angels may not have the resounding confluence or ability that Angel-Mind imbued Salk with, living and developing the gift of Angel-Mind does make each who uses it an Angel. As Angels, identification and ownership of ideas is tossed aside. Every advance in society is owned by all Angels and all representatives of God, who have contributed to every advance that Angel-Minds supporting each other have made. Society and culture are so interwoven with God and Angels who use Angel-Mind that it is impossible to separate the two. Reliance upon Angel-Mind inventions and concepts clearly illustrates how God has encouraged Angel-Mind to develop and people to succeed.

## Clear Communication

The message that each may feel will reveal itself only when the Angel is sure how to communicate it. There may be many starts and stops, delays and frustrations, yet when the time comes, you will be ready. Collaborating with other Angel-Minds may be the spark of inspiration, motivation, and support that will enhance your message and allow a different perspective and application of how to communicate the message clearly. When the mind is ready to access the message that has been building up and programmed since birth, it will come forth. The message may have been entirely designed to wait until joining with another Angel-Mind's idea before being ready to be unveiled. But until you are ready to communicate it as only a true Angel can, your heart will be hesitant. Don't be discouraged; it is your message knowing its time. Continue to work and refine the message by living and experiencing. Continue to work and refine your life. The message will be sent when the message is ready to be sent—when you are ready to deliver it, and not a minute before. You will be ready when it is time. Have faith and trust. When God is ready for the message and knows it needs to be sent, She will enjoy your presentation of it.

## *Finding the Angel Within*

Angel-Mind deals with flourishing and finding a way that each of us will prosper and save ourselves by encouraging individuals to use Angel-Mind. It deals with God's plan and the Angels that can and will change and influence society. Angels and Angel-Mind are all around us, yet many don't realize the potential each individual has and can contribute. Soul work and passions that reveal individual gifts are emphasized, and the holistic health of all will be considered and prioritized.

Society has convinced each individual that they are working against each other, and in that process, individual messages are minimized in their potential. No message too small, no thought too simple, Angel-Mind is something that can and does change society. There is no better Angel Flight than what can be attributed to the success of the soul work of Bill Gates when he started Microsoft. By delivering and achieving a product that was synchronized with society's development, he was able to enjoy the financial rewards of developing a product that was wanted by the populace. Everyone was using his products, which made computer technology surprisingly easy and convenient. After receiving an enormous amount of money for his product, he chose to acknowledge his option of choosing wings.

His choice of Angel-Mind allowed for the Bill and Melinda Gates Foundation to contribute massive amounts of money to improve world health and end disease. He found his Angel-Mind after finding soul work with his passion for computers. The message within was helping to contribute to the health of humanity. After finding success, the soul becomes motivated to contribute and share in an Angel-Mind fashion.

## *The Persistence of Angels*

Angelhood is not an easy job. Being engaged in society's problems and being willing to help when needed is not a particularly easy job. But because God has given this gift of Angel-Mind, it would be a shame to let this world get any worse. As Angel-Mind persists in continually trying to make the difference to the world and those living within it and depending on it, God watches and waits.

## Dividing and Divining Angels in a Secular Society

Angels exist. They have contributed to every cultural advance that has allowed better ideas and higher possibilities of success. Angel-Mind is what brings better living. But the basis of America is secular, logical, and demonstrates a resistance to belief in God and Angels. Undiscovered angels never explore their predisposition for Angel-Mind, or society discourages the discovery of Angel-Mind before the true relationship with God is revealed. Infighting between angels who are loyal to their faith hampers Angel-Mind development and detection of how close we are to God.

Each of us has an Angel Nature that we each must find and nurture so that we can all heal and express God's plans for this world and each other. Instilled by the programs from God and societal advances we have all used and become reliant on, Angel Nature is a calling that we must heed. To contribute our best by protecting each other, leading and supporting one another in this time of need and to turn the tides on what can be considered the truest test of Angelhood: whether we choose to fly when we need to. Not when we want to, but when this earth needs us and God is waiting for us to make the crucial decision of using the wings She gave us. The greatest Watchmaker will smile and wonder what took us so long to heed the call.

Faith in God and Angels is not in high supply. Yet the possibilities exist that show how Angel-Mind can become a dominant societal force. Individuals given the benefit of the doubt may take advantage of it. But the chance must be taken; any individual discovering Angel-Mind can find a moment of transcendence for humanity to choose to unite with God, in the responsibility of helping others and respecting treating this planet with reverence. The methods of waste, corruption, and individualistic achievement have been returned to time and time again. The reason Angel-Mind exists is so that success can nurture God's peoples until we learn how to use Angel-Mind to benefit ourselves and contribute to God's plans.

As Angels, the prayers and support will continue. The wings have got to continue to beat, to support others. When prayers are bolstered with massive energy and acute focus, they do change the reality of the world. Humans are hurting. And yet, many are not ready to connect with God. Angels and the use of Angel-Mind must continue. Addictions are running rampant because of misplaced drives and motivations. Angels continue to stay with humans to fully represent God and the God-Values that will take care of and comfort humans.

Divided by society's denial of the relationship with God and the realization that Angel-Mind unites us all, Angels become distracted when they need to continue to develop their reliance on and use of Angel-Mind. Angels who have found the ultimate faith in their belief have actually found the tenacity to stay with their beliefs and have been able to contribute an incomplete part of God's message. The messages will start to complete themselves once each individual starts using Angel-Mind to reveal their programming, abilities, messages, and goodwill to humankind. It is then that

God and God-Values will guide their flight, and each Angel will contribute to society in their own way.

The differences in Angels' faith and belief are the unique reflections of God's message within the Angel-Mind that is used by that particular Angel's spirit-orientation. An individual's connection to God-Values and reliance on Angels who came before them shows how connected we are to God. God's messages and values relate to contribution, leadership, advocacy, and protection. These behaviors shouldn't just be something that can be noted as influencing behavior; they should be assumed, encouraged to develop, even relied on with the realization of how God and Angel-Mind saturate society. God is not just a belief; it is a reality, as society and culture express their needs and individuals inherently express their ability through Angel-Mind. Still, regardless of the societal discord that may be experienced from believing in God, Angels pray. With each prayer and individual focus, individuals powerfully shift reality.

Quantum physics validates this occurrence. Large amounts of focused energy create events beyond description. Quantum physics shows the possibilities of God and the universe. It relates to the effect of the observer on an event. The Observer Effect shows that your thoughts affect reality. There is a wave of potential that reduces to a focused pattern when watched or observed and the focused energy of prayer is added. By realizing prayer is exactly that focus that changes possibilities, God the Watchmaker and Observer enhances prayers and potentials to become reality. Angels who persist in praying, who believe that they are making a difference, are the reason that the connection to God and Angel-Mind is still here, still changing and reinforcing humanity. By directing an observation, consciousness, and expectations there is a change in how certain realities and the possibilities are distributed! Angels continue to pray, continue to believe. Angel-Mind is displaying the faith and belief that we all need, exist with, and prosper with God.

Dividing angels by differences in a particular faith is losing the forest within the trees. The greatest realization that will bring togetherness is by divining Angel-Mind, not dividing Angel-Mind. The prophecy of God's intent for us is to become the caring Angels who will protect and serve humanity and save this earth and all of God's creations.

Angels continue to believe, continue to put their faith in God and Angel-Mind. Yet many individuals are on such different times of development and understanding of Angel-Mind's dependence on God, with so many different programs, that society is not united. Each Angel can find Angel-Mind manifesting itself in ideas, applications, and inventions. Individuals get to accept the establishment of Angel-Mind and rely on it before the discovery of society's dependence on God, Angels, and Angel-Mind can be realized. Every idea that is groundbreaking, every motivation to do things better, means that Angel-Mind is announcing its presence and the nuances of God's existence in every individual's life. Each person can be assumed to be a beginning representative of God which can nurture and encourage Angel-Mind to grow. Society will succeed by dependence on Angel-Mind and God-Values. We are a society built by Angels, existing and using Angel-Mind, relying on other Angels' advances and contributions. Each Angel-Mind brings completion to God's plan. Examining Angel-Mind and how it will provide a [R]evolution of humanity is the only way that the human race will survive.

God is alive in each of us and is brought about by works of gifted Angels. Understanding that these gifts are given by God's Angel-Mind can be a substantive reason to reintroduce yourself to finding the message that God has activated in your soul. Realizing you are a crucial link for the message you have been made to give is reason to emphasize self-care. By choosing to live in this space, you become present with society's needs, wants, and dependence on your contribution. Choosing to use and develop Angel-Mind is such a rewarding decision; it should be celebrated. This world can be infested with bitter hatred and polarized fear, making the brain's survival instincts go awry. There are so many ways that Angels can be hurt or fight against themselves; it may require great care to be the Angel you can be. But it can also result in so much good. Rather than having each person prove themselves an Angel by their use of Angel-Mind, it needs to be assumed that with support and motivation, those who are predisposed towards Angel-Mind will find the way. We all have access to Angel-Mind when we are each created by God and can demonstrate God-Values in our unique way with a unique perspective of timing and giving. Contribution, leadership, advocacy, and protection are within each of us, and are waiting to be celebrated and displayed.

## *Forgot...or for God?*

Angels persist in trying to offer a better life to those in need. The calling of Angel-Mind resounds by protecting vulnerable areas, or with each forgotten or disenfranchised person that is not being served by society or being allowed to contribute to society. It takes a very receptive and discerning individual to understand the needs of people who have been forgotten by society—people who have lost their way and struggling through tough times, or who are actually just waiting to reunite with society may be sleeping on the street corner, or begging for cash. Their confidence and reliance on their message within have been altered by some experience that shook their faith. It may be time to find a message by observing how you feel you can contribute or help. It is time to realize that the people who are forgotten are the people that Angel-Mind wants to include, support in a helpful way, and remember. The supportive and leadership-oriented Angel-Mind can see this and will know what to do.

As I was walking the streets of my city, a homeless man was sleeping on the sidewalk. I stopped, completed a God Circuit, and wished this Angel the best that I could. His contribution of his existence was enough for me to accept this gift. I had an appointment I had to get to, so I left without actually altering the situation at all, but I will remember him in my prayers.

By remembering him that night, I changed and reprocessed my pathways. He is not just a forgotten person. I allow myself to change my regard for this individual and may work to understand how I can work to better serve this city's homeless population. I program my Angel-Mind with God's language of prayer. Every face has a message from God, and it is time to start to see and depend on those messages.

## Darkening Skies

We must accept the realization that whatever our Angel-Mind, no matter how much goodness we plan to do or resolute goodness it has, it is affected by the experiences and outcomes of our life. These experiences change outcomes and manifest in some experiences that were never planned for. Experiencing frequent failures will harm the tendency to try again, even though the next try will be the breakthrough. I realize that even as I am trying to operate with Angel-Mind and contribute my message and protect the vulnerable, my programs oppose each other. These programs are telling me that I'm a protector and I need to protect as many identities as I can, yet I question who I'm protecting. Dark conditions may mask our true purpose and not allow a steadfast flight. The subject matter I'm going to talk about may cause some people decide to turn off their attention. My programs are telling me to stop, that I must not disclose the identity of the person who changed my life forever.

I have prayed over this, and my prayers have let me know this: behavior is controlled by the mind, and things that occur within the mind show behavior that will happen again. But I also realize the complex web of societal readiness affecting the acceptance of my message. The impulses will return to the individual and will likely become more apparent to the individual who abused me as they get older and their mind continues to fail in representing God's message of protection and contribution. I must make sure that another is not abused like I was.

The thing that ultimately changed my path and message with my Angel-flight was the rape and molestation that I experienced from fifth grade through my senior year of college. This not only speaks to the programming of my sexuality throughout my youth, adolescence, and adulthood, it reflects how I was continually manipulated to bring pleasure to my abuser. This long-term trauma has not only harmed me in every way; it also reflects the abuser's continued reliance on using illegitimate means from which they will achieve an amount of pleasure. I have been silenced until now, when I found my wings. Every Angel has a challenge and the gift to overcome that challenge. And I look to protect those that I can with my Angel-Mind.

Understanding the hypothalamus is a major predictor of how an individual will regulate the activities of fighting, fleeing, feeding, and mating. I can make a prediction that it will happen again. I cannot let this horrible experience happen and affect another's message. But I wait for the chance for my message to have the cultural significance it needs.

My life changed forever. I cannot think of a time when I did not experience the deleterious effects of the event. I look at how my whole life changed in those moments, how the extreme sexuality was present in my life from that moment on. How my whole potential changed, from someone who was ready to change society with my passion and heart, to someone who struggles with depression and who blames himself for what he's been through. The length of my abuse has caused an extreme form of trauma known as Complex-PTSD. Alterations in self, meaning, emotional regulation, and relational variables are influenced when experiencing long-term trauma. But I remember, every Angel has a challenge and a gift to get past that challenge. Right now, I find myself depending on that gift of Angel-Mind.

My potential was never reached. Chances to deliver and even discover my message were never taken. I was hurt and the painful echoes of the abuse resound in my body and soul and deafen my potential. My soul damaged, the environment of my world changed. Most of all, how I approved of myself and how I regarded others changed. But now, I've rediscovered my wings. I fly again, maybe not with the same abilities or possibility, but with a stronger message.

I am grateful that I have gone through this, because I'm not sure how anyone else could solve this problem: studies show that rapists will rape again, and I cannot let that happen. I will not let another individual be robbed of the protection they deserve because of my inaction. The hypothalamus expresses needs and motivations that is internal. The pathway of my abuser needs to be stopped, re-educated, or at the very least monitored because the steps they take they may not be aware of.

But I balk at the opportunity to care for others. The statute of limitations has run out on this crime. And the amount of inconvenience for me to bring this up now in my life is very difficult. But I must protect others from the experiences that I have lived through. It is difficult, with experiences of programming and silent subservience affecting me. But I will not let anyone else go through this without trying to contribute what I can and bringing this into the spotlight.

## *A Steady Flight*

My path and message are chosen. I will not let anyone else go through this. I am grateful, because this story needs to be told and I'm not sure who else could tell this. It brings me fulfillment to know that I am doing the best I can to contribute my message within my soul and to protect those who I can with the four attributes of Angel-Mind. I am contributing to the discourse pertaining to sexual abuse and protection of vulnerable people. I have survived this to make sure no one else gets hurt by the same thing.

Angel-Mind enables my considering protecting the person that abused me and protecting those that could be affected. I am not ready to stop. I will continue to stay vigilant, continue to realize that while the statute of limitations may have expired, that may mean my abuser has just gotten better at hiding the behavior which negatively impacted my life. Rapists will rape again, yet Angel-Mind never stops protecting the people that need protection. Protecting others is how I have been programmed, which extends even to my abuser, and yet, I realize that to protect others, I'm going to have to make sure this individual doesn't rape again by disclosing an identity. I question whether my programs of protection extend to the person who raped me. This conundrum is one of the most hard-hitting of my existence. No one said being an Angel is easy, right? The sobering reality is that as individuals get older, they return to more of themselves. And I can't let the ruinous experiences of rape and sexual abuse happen to another. I'm looking for some way to protect those who need it. When the culture is ready, that is when my message will help others. I may never be the Angel that God first planned on and created me to be, but I can be the Angel that I am.

# THE [R]EVOLUTION

## Becoming

Angel-Mind has been away from this earth and God's creations for almost too long. We have all stood by silently and watched this earth and its conditions become unrecognizable to those whom have the faith in God and who are Angels. A wasteland of corruption, of thievery, and an illustration of what a world looks like without the combining force of God is becoming a refuse of unrecognized responsibilities and corruption. As Angels, we shall know our glory and Angel-Mind will have been achieved when no one on this earth is needing. Addictions are quelled when each individual knows what they need to do and that their contributions are appreciated.

Acceptance of Angel-Mind responsibility is a gift to be celebrated, because it is what each individual is made to do as they realize and reveal the messages that God has made to grow within them. Attention starts to expand when realizing higher processing opportunities. Angel-Mind becomes a force that connects and rejoins humanity with God.

Each Angel-Mind will be celebrated as an answer to a developing question that God has created each of us to solve. The dimensions of reality will shift to represent a true spiritual approach to answering the world's problems. Each Angel will contribute a solution to a problem that has developed or is developing. Angel-Mind will resonate with the passion, education, and learning it was built for. The truest form of being with Angel-Mind is the choice to become and to contribute. It is the choice to put the work in, to share messages of saving the earth and all of God's creations. Because it is time, Angels. It is time.

The product of Angel-Mind that will save humanity and reconnect us as people who protect and serve each other is reliance on God and finding the gifts of Angel-Mind within—finding the gifts that can contribute, provide healing, and stop the hurting reflects the importance of discovering Angel-Mind. The actions that are taken when resonating with Angel-mind will enable a system that is dependent on each other and will be one of the most intricate and complicated achievements of humanity—a system of contribution and interconnection, where each one of us feels that together we will save the world.

According to brain scientists, reprocessing trauma happens through the cerebrum. By knowing I have others to protect, by knowing others are needing me, I give myself the reprocessing that it takes to overcome the disconnect and numbing that I have to deal with. I give myself life, as I find God within my Angel-Mind. By being with and supporting others, trauma is healed in the people that are supported.

Humanity has found an optimal form that has allowed them to thrive in the conditions they are in. Humans have accepted the levels of skills and abilities within them sufficient to live the best they can. By including different examples of Angel-Mind through this book, I have shown how Angel-Mind has contributed to society and is related to societal enhancement by concentrating on God-Values and divinity. Role models who have used Angel-Mind and God-Values to contribute to this earth's wellness have shown the way to better living. Each individual must continue to develop Angel-Mind concepts and God-Values in the way it was originally developed by God for, to allow humans to develop into Angels that can take care of humans, enhance living, and protect their earthly paradise. Environmental damage and killing the earth's species, overpopulation, and disenfranchisement of people—is that the only way there is to live? Or is there another way that evolutionary changes haven't been able to address? Because this [R]evolution just doesn't happen with evolutionary changes like the shape of a beak or better camouflage; this evolution of humanity is a [R]evolution of reprocessing through the old parts of the brain and finding new behaviors in the newest parts of the brain--allowing a final part of evolution to be completed and the Angels and Angel-Mind programmed within us to finally be accessed.

If successful, we may be the first species in this universe that has achieved Angelhood, pulling ourselves from the brink of extinction. And as God looks from His Watchmaking, a smile will form on that beautiful face. God will know that the intricate series of double helixes that were constructed which allowed the [R]evolution of His Angels. God continues to smile, watch, and wait to see how many more combinations of programs will allow the saving of this world. Because each of us, working, protecting, and depending on each other, contributing our best to each other, will be smiling. The individuals that have struggled so hard to survive will be the group of Angels that support and protect each other. And that is the biggest secret of Angel- Mind, of humanity, and our survival. We each bring a better representation of God when we are together.

## ANGELS REMEMBER: ISN'T IT TIME FOR GABRIELLE'S LAW?

The contributions and advances and flights of particular Angels who have demonstrated amazing leadership and advocacy for those that need it are reliant upon the culture they live in to help complete their message. President Kennedy was one of those angels. He realized that a specific population could benefit from integration with people who accepted the responsibility of caring and advocating for those experiencing mental illness. As Angel-Mind users, the realization that integration of different types of people is needed for people to heal can be accepted. It takes big concepts like Angel-Mind to take a subject like mental illness and look at the best health practices that will change individuals' lives. I wrote this about the mental health crisis in America to demonstrate the essential part that America could play in healing others. Forgotten and unnoticed by many as the concept of deinstitutionalization working, Angels find the wings ready to realize this is a group of people who have almost been forgotten…but not by God-Values, who prioritize the support of individuals in need! It picks up with the shooting of Gabrielle Giffords at a political event:

The sad fact about the recent shooting of Gabrielle Giffords in Tucson, Arizona, is that her trauma and now inspiring recovery, no matter how courageous it may be, didn't have to happen. It is only a reminder of the incomplete rehabilitation picture for many Americans experiencing mental illness.

The shooter of Gabrielle Giffords was mentally ill and experiencing schizophrenia. He was probably one of four million untreated schizophrenics in the US. Mental Illness has been affecting America's landscape long enough—the Arizona incident with shootings and other acts of homicide or desperation. Virginia, California, Georgia, and Wisconsin are just a few of the states affected by shootings. Recent shootings in Fort Lauderdale and Illinois both took students' lives. The Columbine and Virginia Tech school shootings are two of the more publicized and notorious incidents of individuals acting out, screaming for our help–yet we were not prepared to listen.

The sad fact is that the deinstitutionalization that America prides itself on is not working because it has not been completed. See the homeless people on the side of the road begging for cash? Others who sleep on the park benches and don't have a place to call home? Chances say the people are struggling against some trauma, life challenges they cannot meet, or some other sort of mental illness where they are existing without their needs being met, facing begging or homelessness as the only way to be. America is not stepping up to serve those affected by mental illness, and we are paying the price.

The first stage of deinstitutionalization—getting the people with mental illnesses out of the hospitals—was done, but the second stage, designed to provide care for and supervision of seriously ill people living in the community was never completed. The 1963 Community Mental Health Centers Act was designed for this integral part of caring for those dealing with mental illness. This act sought to close down the giant state hospitals that were providing only supervisory care, not treatment, with the presupposition that their patients would be transferred from the state hospitals to community-based care. The transition to community hospitals was a more mentally healthy approach to treatment. It appeared better, safer, and a more independent setting for people with mental illnesses. It was a perfect setting for the recovery of individuals, except many neighborhoods didn't want the mentally ill in their neighborhoods.

The mentally ill are not having their needs met, and they are also a displaced group that is unwanted by many individuals. America has the blueprint for caring for these misunderstood and stigmatized individuals, in the form of President Kennedy's Act, and shouldn't waste any time. This is the time and the place, and it carries the momentum lawmakers may need to consider this as an effort to address completion of the second act of deinstitutionalization. This action can be a step to a healthier, more caring America.

Dollars and cents are what usually drives most laws, and mental illness affects a much bigger percentage of the population than what most of us can imagine, making it more costly for treatment possibilities. Is it possible to ask that America work on an already seemingly defunct act that has not ever been completed, which many people will assume is working "just fine"? Most definitely;

as the populace of America continues to grow, more people will be affected by mental illness, more behaviors caused by mental illness will affect each member of society, and every person will be looking for some way to treat mental illness and control those situations. Misunderstandings and misassumptions about the mentally ill are not the only problems with mental illness when needs are not met. Violence must also be assumed to be a response option for those who have been untreated and unsupervised. Looking at schizophrenia, one of the causes of the nation's homicidal acts and behavior, there is a realization of responsibility and care. It represents only one category of violent mental illness. How many illnesses will need to be treated and cared for, representing a huge initial cost for Americans in this time of economic hardship?

Is it financially possible to consider applying Kennedy's Act to each state? In fact, some states already use a version of the act. The state of New York has already enacted a law called Kendra's Law, which provides for court-ordered outpatient treatment. A patient can be committed to an inpatient hospital stay and mandated to outpatient treatment and monitoring.

Is it the right time to complete an act that was never fully carried out for a group of people that are unable to always find a voice? As society becomes more processing-intensive and more education is needed to fully function in culture, isn't it time to look at providing for those experiencing mental illness with their needs and monitoring their progress? Mental illness has gotten our attention; now the big question will be whether we're prepared to listen and do what is needed to help those that are affected by mental illness.

Kendra's Law was an attempt of New York State to address the needs of the growing problem of mental illness in New York. Isn't it time for Gabrielle's Law to finally complete President Kennedy's 1963 Act to fulfill the needs of a struggling population across the country who are dealing with mental Illness? Haven't we waited long enough?

As Angels, we want to help those who need it. And this is the time to consider helping an underserved and unrepresented group of people who need us. And as an Angel, a smile forms on my face as the wings we have can show we will lift a group of people who need help by our God-Values of contribution, leadership, advocacy, and protection.

## Angel-Mind Overcoming Trauma

Individuals who have experienced trauma are dealing with one of the biggest challenges in their life when trying to engage it without using Angel-Mind. Trauma can be the biggest detractor to life and finding the message from God within. The brain stem and its survival motivation can react to traumatic memories and environments in a survival mode. Healing trauma concerns transferring the trauma resonance interfering with the brain stem's survival motivation and reprocessing it through Angel-Mind. Angel-Mind can reprocess the deadly meaning of trauma and transform it to a meaning that is not conflicting with the motivations and ultimate concerns of the brain stem.

When trauma interferes with the brain stem's frequencies of survival, it causes various psychological and physiological symptoms. When the [R]evolution of Angel-Mind deals more with healing trauma through support, individuals will find freedom with their wings. Changing these symptoms by reprocessing with Angel-Mind is the true way to trauma recovery. Becoming a true Angel of God by using Angel-Mind to its best ability finds outlets for contribution, leadership, advocacy, and protection.

Frustration of Angel-Mind processes can easily happen as a survivor of trauma and their brain undergo the changes that trauma produces. An injury to the brain actually reduces access to Angel-Mind because the brain senses threats in its environment and rewires to represent a sensory predisposition to attend to any other threats.

Deep breathing can restore Angel-Mind ability by retuning the disruptive frequencies of trauma and resetting stress levels. No longer is the brain running strictly by its senses; it is finding the ability to fly by using the currents of the breath.

Reprocessing trauma can be your choice of how best to express how you want to change trauma's hold on your internal and external world. But the choice to change trauma will rest in Angel-Mind's and God's connection. Prayer and introspection will reveal the methods that will enable you to deal with and heal with your trauma. Finding support groups dealing with your specific trauma, talking about it, and forming secure and supportive relationships will promote healing. Angel-Mind inspires those relationships that form together in caring and wellness.

God will encourage healing from trauma with the wonderful Angels that are brought into your life and the Angel-Mind that can reprocess the trauma that can seem uncontrollable. Angel-Mind and God can control the trauma: they can help you reprocess the feelings you are experiencing to become a more representative expression of who you are. God can nurture you and can heal the traumatic experience within you, yet trying to reprocess the trauma into something Angel-Mind and the brain stem can both work with is going to happen only when you, God, and Angel-Mind are ready.

## *A Silent Angel*

As I bring my hands together in prayer, as I ask God to make me an Angel so that I can support the people and things that God has made, try to make changes that will enhance the quality of life for humanity, and revere and respect the earth. My abuse forewarns that my abuser does not understand what they are doing or have done. Yet I am not alone; others will step up to the challenge as well. Angel-Mind has been encouraged and freed to do what it is designed to. Changes in society need to be made. I am blessed that I can realize these things, and that God has given my Angel-Mind wings. God did not plan on the anomalies of abuse or accidents that have affected my possibilities. But God does place ultimate faith in the Angel-Mind that I use and the

God-Values I adhere to.

The trauma that I have experienced has silenced many of my abilities, but I continue to find my message that God has planted within me. I continue to pray. I do feel the heightened stress levels that show in children who have been abused. And these stress levels plant an urgency that I need to get this story and my message out to warn others and begin a national dialogue about how sexual abuse can be prevented. I need my story to be a testimonial to how the story of sexual abuse has been accepted too long. And as an Angel, I will do my best to bring God-Values to be the solution. I will pray and continue to find and wait for my developing message of contribution, leadership, advocacy, and protection. I have been blessed with the knowledge and realization of how important Angel-Mind and God are to the human race, because I know that Angel-Mind will play a part in saving those that use it. And even those that don't, but who need its protection, advocacy, and leadership, will be assisted by Angel-Mind's myriad applications. Because we all are reliant on seeing each other and God that connects us to save ourselves.

Neurologists say that exposure to sex at too young an age actually can influence addictive tendencies. Many thoughts originating from the rape and molestation are not my own. By recognizing this, I bring God-ritual into my life until the thought dissipates. I program my Angel-Mind with the connection that will overcome what I have experienced. When God is ready for me to overcome the struggle, Angel-Mind will deal with it no more. The precise timing of God's message of me finding my gifts to overcome my challenges is what I trust. The message and values that God has given me will prepare me to succeed. I have quite a long road of self-discovery, self-boundaries, and compassion that I must learn to survive. And while the partnership of Angel-Mind and God is a great companionship to walk and be with, the road is long and the conditions that I will travel through will be tough. But will there ever be a greater travelling companion than to exist with God and use Angel-Mind? I smile and I am grateful. This trip will continue my message that is needed by this world. Because there is no greater solution than Angel-Mind contributing to where we are at than being an agent of change ourselves.

## Discovering the Inner Angel

Each individual who hears of Angel-Mind can have definite reactions to it. Either they disbelieve it, or they can find themselves asking, "Why haven't I been aware of this concept before and the advantages it brings me and all of the world's inhabitants?" The experiences you have lived through may have obscured the vision of your message and your realization of humanity's potential. Or the contributions of other Angel-Minds have made living so easy, that by relying on other Angels' discoveries and inventions, the question has never come up. But with the question of using Angel-Mind inside of you and the yearning of Angel-Mind to connect with God, Angel-Mind experiences are encouraged. The greatness of this society and culture is on display, the glory of operating with

Angel-Mind and our collaboration with God in how we affect this world, and Angel-Mind is what will encourage it. There's only one last step for you: contribute all the glorious things that God has programmed within you and how your experiences have interacted with the environment. It's time to contribute, be yourself, and find that message within and develop your Angel-Mind by living and striving for higher processing, while encouraging others' Angel-Minds to manifest. Because the watch is being completed and the greatest Watchmaker is just waiting for you. And smiling. And watching.

Is it our time to truly use Angel-Mind and become the Angels that can save the earth and its inhabitants? To become so encouraging, protective, and supportive of the individuals on this earth who can benefit from it? And we all can benefit from it. We each have the capability to use God's message and values within us, and we each need to connect to Angel-Mind. We each need to become the Angels that we are made to be and allow ourselves to resonate with God's message. We each are the solution to the world's problems. The invitation has been made because our awareness has extended to every solution we can give to this world. And each of us Angels, we've got some God-work to do. It's time to find that Divine Contribution that we each have to give. God waits, and smiles, and realizes that each Angel-Mind has been constructed for the purpose of saving the world and its inhabitants. What are we waiting for, Angels? It's time to find the wings God has given us and use them.

www.ingramcontent.com/pod-product-compliance
Lightning Source LLC
Chambersburg PA
CBHW050504110426
42742CB00018B/3364